SPALDING®

Youth League Football Coaching and Playing

TOM FLORES
& BOB O'CONNOR

MASTERS PRESS
A Division of Howard W. Sams & Co.

Published by Masters Press (A Division of Howard W. Sams)
2647 Waterfront Pkwy. E. Dr., Suite 300,
Indianapolis, IN 46214

Published 1993.

Printed in the United States of America.

Library of Congress Cataloging-in-Publication Date

Flores, Tom

Youth league football : coaching and playing / Tom Flores and Bob O'Conner.

p. cm. -- (Spalding sports library)

At head of title: Spalding.

ISBN 0-940279-69-X : $12.95

1. Youth league football--Coaching. I. O'Connor, Robert, 1932-.

II. Title. III. Series.

GV959.6.F57 1993

796.332'07'7--dc20 93-14323

CIP

Credits:

Front cover photo of Ryan Harpold taken by Stephen Baker.

Background photo provided by the Indianapolis Colts.

Cover design by Michele Holden.

Interior photos of Drew Black, John Dillon, Lyle Young, and Adam Hoog taken by Stephen Baker.

Photography consultation provided by Mark Montieth.

Text Design by Leah Marckel.

The Better Sports for Kids Program

The Better Sports for Kids program is the proud mission of the National Youth Sports Coaches Association (NYSCA) which was created in 1981 to help improve out-of-school sports for over 20 million youth under the age of 16.

The non-profit association's staff of professionals work to implement a variety of programs, all in cooperation with national, state, and local associations.

The Better Sports for Kids program and its wide range of services help parents and kids get the most out of their participation in youth sports through programs such as the National Youth Sports Coaches Association national certification program for coaches, the National Association of Youth Leagues which helps leagues with all their needs in running a youth league organization, the All-American Drug-Free Team program which joins coaches and players in a drug education and prevention program, and the early introduction to lifetime sports through programs such as Hook a Kid on Golf.

The NYSCA is pleased to endorse the Spalding Youth League Series as an informative selection of coaching materials for youth coaches who wish to provide quality instruction and promote self esteem on and off the playing field.

Foreword

Youth sports are a great way for parents to spend time with their children. Fathers, mothers, sons, and daughters can all benefit from their participation in sports, and coaching a youth league team may be one of the most beneficial experiences that a parent can share with his or her child.

Youth coaches must be able to teach the skills necessary to play the game effectively and safely, but they must also realize how important they are to the children that they teach. Coaches often take the place of absent or busy parents. They must realize that the game is fun, but that the children are the most important part of the activity. The game offers ways to educate them, but the children must be the coaches' main concern.

The fascination of the American public with football makes the sport a natural choice for your child's participation. Because it is played at so many different levels and widely televised at the collegiate and professional levels, parents can not only work with their children to develop their skills, but also watch games with them to foster an appreciation of the sport and a bond between parent and child that can last a lifetime.

As your child learns more about football skills and executing them properly, he will become more interested in the game. The skills should be taught when the child is properly motivated to learn that skill. By timing your teaching, both you and your child will enjoy the experience.

Always remember, the most important aspect of youth football is FUN!!

Acknowledgements

Grateful acknowledgment to Jim Bush, track coach at U.S.C. and former coach at U.C.L.A. and running coach for the L.A. Raiders and the L.A. Dodgers, for all of his help with the information on speed development.

Thanks also to Ben Agajanian, one of the finest kickers of all time and the nation's premier kicking coach, for all of his help with the chapter on punt and kick fundamentals.

Table of Contents

league Youth FOOTBALL

I. Coaching Children

You, as a parent or as a coach, want to do the best you can for the child or teenager with whom you are working. To do your best, you should ask yourself a few questions to make sure you understand your goals. These questions should be kept in mind whether working with your own child or the children of others.

- Does the child really want to be there?
- Is the teaching directed to the age of the players?
- Is the activity fun for the children?

How can the skills and theories be taught effectively? Remember that play is one of the most important aspects of a child's life. Don't kill his or her spirit with "work." Don't kill your spirit either. Even as adults, we must keep that youthful outlook and attitude of play.

Does the child really want to be there? Not every child has the innate temperament to enjoy playing football at a competitive level, but everyone should be able to enjoy some of the skills associated with football. Passing, catching, running, kicking, and agility drills can be fun for every young child — boy or girl.

Although children may enjoy and benefit from the time spent learning to do shoulder rolls, catch, and throw, parents and coaches must realize that, as children grow older, they may prefer basketball, computers, or playing the piano. Children should be encouraged to experiment with every area of human development, including academics, sports, and the arts, to find the area that most appeals to them.

The decision to pursue an activity belongs to the children. Is this what they really want to do? Will they look back on the experience and be glad that they participated, or will they remember it as something they were "made" to do? Is the teaching directed to the age of the players? Some parents and youth coaches seem to think that kids are smaller versions of themselves, with the same bodies and brains. The parent or youth coach who tries to teach a young boy or girl to throw a curve ball doesn't understand that the young person's bones are still soft near the elbow joint. The wrist snap involved in throwing a curve ball can permanently injure the elbow and make it impossible for that child to pitch when he or she reaches high school.

Parents and coaches should go slowly with their teaching. You certainly don't want to work on the technique for the "seven-step passing drop" with kindergartners. Plan your teaching so that it is enjoyable and so that the skills learned are both safe and appropriate for the age of your players.

Your major goal should not be to teach the children football, but to teach them *through* football. While it is enjoyable to see your players succeed at any level of play, from Pop Warner to the professional level, you must keep sight of the fact that making your players into mature happy adults should be your primary goal. Remember the words of the philosopher Santayana, "Fanaticism consists of redoubling your effort when you have forgotten your aim."

Is the activity fun for the children?

We all learn better when we enjoy what we are learning. Throwing and catching may seem to be enjoyable at any age, but learning pass-protection blocking or pass-rush techniques will not be a lot of fun unless the boy sees the need for it in playing organized football. The amount of enjoyment the team takes from learning a sport depends on the amount and type of discipline that the team has.

Discipline is essential to achievement in any area of life. Discipline can be intrinsic (self-directed) or extrinsic (imposed from the outside). It can be positive or negative. Parents and teachers sometimes motivate children with negative extrinsic discipline — punishment and "put-downs." In fact, some people think that "discipline" means being punished.

Intrinsic discipline occurs when an individual wants to do something, either to please himself or a parent or teacher. When you make learning fun, the activity becomes an intrinsic motivation. Have you ever seen kids voluntarily playing catch or kicking a ball? Of course! They are intrinsically motivated to have fun. The same principle applies to reading or writing. If a child enjoys sports, he is more likely to want to read if the reading material is a sports book.

Extrinsic discipline is imposed from an outside source. If parents say they will buy their child an ice cream cone if he catches eight-of-ten passes, that is a positive extrinsic discipline. If they say their son has to do 20 push-ups if he misses two passes, that is a negative extrinsic discipline. Spanking or chastising a player is also a negative extrinsic discipline.

So often with parents and coaches, discipline is primarily negative. They yell at their players and assign extra laps or push-ups as punishment. Not only does this decrease the enjoyment of the participants, but it also makes things that are good for the players, like running and push-ups, have a negative connotation.

Psychologists know that positive intrinsic discipline is the most effective and that negative extrinsic discipline is the least effective. Therefore, the best way to get your players to play hard and well is to make practice enjoyable and to develop in your team the desire to play. Make it fun.

When you are teaching, the most effective method of keeping your players motivated and interested is to compliment them on what they are doing right. The less effective method is to negatively criticize them, but the worst method of all is to not say anything to your players. When you help your players, tell them what they are doing right. Make corrections when necessary to help them to improve. Teach them with love and they will enjoy it; continually criticize them, and their desire will disappear.

Making it enjoyable

The younger the child, the more important it is that a practice activity be enjoyable. As children grow older, they become able to delay gratification and realize that working out in the spring will help them to be a better player in the fall. Young children can't see that far ahead. They want to have fun now by throwing, catching, jumping, and getting praise from their parents and coaches.

Many experts believe that children today have been overexposed to organized athletics at too early an age. With soccer, baseball, football and basketball seasons overlapping one another, there is little time for "Hide and Seek" or "Cowboys and Indians." We find quite often that, by the time these over-organized kids have entered high school, they have had enough of organized sports and are less likely to participate. The number of candidates for high school teams in both football and basketball has dwindled as the youth sports leagues have grown.

Don't push your children too hard. Help them enjoy learning and want to work with you. Kids who have fathers, mothers, and youth coaches who want to spend time with them in non-threatening play are much more likely to continue with sports because they realize that sports are fun.

How can the skills and theories be taught most effectively?

Start with where your players are physiologically and psychologically. Are they ready to learn to play catch, or kick a ball?

Physiologically, the bones are soft at the ends until the boy is fully grown, which occurs somewhere between the ages of 15 and 21.

A major principle of teaching and coaching is to make certain that the kids want to learn. Start with something they enjoy. Boys generally want to spend time with their fathers or other adult males, so just getting to be with them is fun. The same can be true for younger girls. For the younger kids, stick to throwing, catching, and kicking games. Give plenty of compliments.

When working with a young child, keep it simple. Merely playing catch or showing him or her how to do a forward roll is enough. Reaching perfection in fundamentals before the eighth birthday is not important; there is plenty of time.

Emphasize the keys to learning that are in this book. These keys are a product of over sixty years of coaching experience, and they work at every level of football. Believe it or not, professional players still need instruction on how to catch and throw a football. The glamour of the game starts with the perfection of fundamentals in practice ... every day. An old saying, "chance favors the prepared mind," applies to football. With proper fundamentals, success is much more likely.

Remember that you are working with players for yourself as well as for them. These precious moments will live with you always, because nothing is better remembered than the hours spent helping children.

II. The Safety Factors You Must Consider

Growing children and teenagers are prone to certain types of injuries. The responsible parent or coach must be aware of these concerns so that temporary or permanent problems do not develop.

Injuries to the Bones

The bones in an adult skeleton are hard. Children's bones are soft, however, so that they can grow. They do not totally harden until the child is finished growing, anywhere from the early teens to the early twenties.

The most common bone problem for boys is a condition known as Osgood-Schlatter's. Estimates are that as many as 90 percent of boys have some evidence of this problem. In Osgood-Schlatter's, the tendon that attaches the muscle of the front of the thigh (the quadriceps) into the leg, just below the knee, pulls out on the upper leg bone. This is not only painful, but also causes a permanent bump just below the knee cap. The condition is rare in girls.

The normal activities of children, such as running and jumping, are the major causes of this condition. Heavy weight training using the quadriceps at too early an age also can cause or aggravate the condition.

Broken bones are usually not much of a problem. Kids have fallen off bikes and out of trees for years, and they usually recover fully.

Injuries to the Ligaments

The bones are held together by pieces of tough material called ligaments. When these ligaments are stretched, we call it a sprain. Stretched ligaments take years to shrink back to their original size and some never do.

Many times a sprained ankle keeps getting resprained. Because the ligament does not immediately return to its original length, the outside of the foot isn't held up as high as it was before the injury. Therefore, the ankle is vulnerable to be sprained again and again. Sprains can be greater problems than breaks over the long run because they often do not heal completely.

Preventing Sprained Ankles

Sprained ankles can be prevented by having your players wear ankle braces or by taping the ankles correctly. Recent evidence indicates that some of the available braces work better than tape and are cheaper in the long run. High top shoes may also have some effect on reducing the ability of the ankle to be sprained.

Strengthening the muscles that hold the foot up might slightly reduce the chance of spraining the ankle. To exercise these muscles, push down with your hand on the outside of the foot (near the little toe), then bring the foot upward against the pressure of the hand.

Preventing Sprained Wrists

It is more difficult to prevent wrist sprains. Two arm bones attach to the eight wrist bones, which attach to five hand bones. This accumulation of bones requires a large number of ligaments to hold the bones together, and, as the wrist can move in so many directions, it is continuously in a position in which it can be sprained. With the increased use of the hands in offensive blocking, the wrists become even more likely to be injured. The best prevention is to wrap a few layers of athletic training tape around the wrist to help support the ligaments.

Preventing Knee Injuries

Knee injuries can be prevented by doing exercises that strengthen the muscles that move the knee joint and by wearing shoes that do not have cleats that anchor the foot to the ground. Exercises for the knee will be discussed in the weight training chapter.

One of the major causes of knee injuries is that the cleats of the shoe anchor the foot to the ground. If the boy is hit from the side, the knee must take the brunt of the hit. If the foot were able to slide or twist on the ground, the force of the blow to the knee would be reduced.

Tennis shoes without cleats, or Tanel shoes with cleats in a circle that enable the foot to turn, are the safest types of shoes.

The circular pattern of cleats in the Tanel shoe allows the foot to spin if a player is hit from the side. This reduces or eliminates the potential injury to a knee.

Another way to protect the knee is to reduce the stress on it by reducing the amount of full speed running, jumping, and heavy weight lifting. Whenever there is a great deal of stress on the muscles of the front of the thigh (the quadriceps), the stress is transferred throughout the knee tendon (the patellar tendon) and into the top of the lower leg bone where the tendon is attached.

Preventing Shoulder Injuries

Strengthening the muscles around the shoulder is the best way to prevent shoulder injuries. Proper technique in performing the fundamentals and learning how to fall correctly are also very important. You should be sure to teach your players to never fall with straight arms. Teaching them to bend their elbows ensures that they will absorb part of the force of the fall with their arms.

Preventing Elbow Injuries

The same preventive measures for preventing shoulder injuries apply to the elbows. Make sure your players practice falling so that bending their arms when they catch themselves becomes second nature. However, developing the biceps muscle is also important as it reduces the chance of dislocating the elbow.

Injuries to the Muscles

Muscle injuries can be reduced by beginning each practice with a proper warm-up and stretching routine and by encouraging your players to develop muscular strength.

Nobody, particularly younger children, should play when injured, but at the higher levels of competition bumps and bruises are part of the game. Playing with pain is part of the development of the "toughness" that is essential to the game. Certainly chapped lips and the like aren't enough to stop anyone from practicing!

The Warm-up

While children are less prone to muscle injuries than adults, they still should learn to use proper warm-ups. The more intense the practice, the greater the need for a proper warm-up.

Start the warm-up by having your players jog while swinging or circling their arms. This will warm up the muscles of the legs. Jumping jacks will warm up the muscles that pull apart and bring together the legs (technically called abduction and adduction).

After the heart rate has increased and the blood flow to the muscles is improved, stretching can begin. Certain muscles should be stretched before an extensive practice session:

The thigh muscles, for running

The chest muscles, for blocking, tackling, or throwing the ball

The lower back muscles, for blocking, tackling, or running with power

The upper back muscles, for tackling The triceps (the back of the upper arms), for throwing and blocking

The calf muscles, for running and jumping

The fingers, for passing and catching

Flexibility

Flexibility is generally defined as the range of motion of a joint. All athletes need a certain amount of flexibility. Stretching exercises should be done slowly.The stretches should be held for for 20 to 30 seconds.

The Flexibility Warm-up

A few simple flexibility exercises should be done before and after every workout or game. They will stretch your players' connective tissues and muscles, which improves reaction time and reduces the risk of injury. The ideal order for stretching exercises is as follows:

Shoulder Rotation. The players stand erect with their arms extended. They then rotate the arms forward in circles with their hands making circles of 12 to 15 inches in diameter. After 15 seconds, they rotate backward for 15 seconds.

Chest Stretch. The players bring their arms up to shoulder level and bend them at the elbow. Have the kids pull the elbows backward until they feel a strong stretch in the upper part of the chest. Hold for 30 seconds.

Chest stretch

Groin Stretch. While sitting on the floor, the players put the soles of their feet together and pull them toward their hips with their hands. With straight backs, have them try to press their knees to the floor. Do this for 30 seconds.

Lower Back and Hamstrings. While sitting on the floor, the players spread their legs outward as far as possible. While keeping their backs and legs straight, and with their toes pointed up, have the players reach as far as possible toward their right ankles. After 30 seconds, have them reach for their left ankles for 30 seconds.

Trunk Twist. The players sit on the ground with their legs straight. Each bends his right leg and crosses it over his left leg. The right foot should be flat on the ground. Each then reaches his left arm around the bent leg as if he were trying to touch his hip. The right arm should be placed behind him as he slowly twists his head and neck until he is looking over their right shoulder. Hold for 30 seconds and then repeat the exercise to the other side.

Thigh and Groin Stretch. From a standing position, have your players step forward with their left leg. Then they should lean forward over their left legs while keeping their left feet flat on the ground. They will then push down with the right leg until they feel a good stretch in the thigh and groin area. (Hands are allowed on the floor for balance.) Continue this stretch for 30 seconds and then repeat to the other side.

III. Developing Agility

Coaches say that football is a game of movement and contact. Players must be able to move quickly in a game. They must know how to move their feet and bodies to avoid some contact or to be on balance when contact will occur. To execute these skills, players must have a great deal of agility so that they can:

- step over players
- fall correctly and be able to quickly regain their feet and continue to play
- continue to maintain contact while blocking
- move past a blocker while pass rushing
- avoid tacklers while running or passing
- free themselves from a defensive back while running a pass pattern
- perform most other movements that occur during a game

Agility Drills

The drills to develop agility should be fun. For example, kids often do somersaults while playing. A somersault, or forward roll, is a basic drill for football. It helps the player to learn to fall while running and then get up and continue to play. Shoulder rolls have similar objectives.

Running with the knees high also is an enjoyable activity that helps a player's speed. This exercise also helps prepare a player to be able to step over others as he runs with the ball, blocks for the ball carrier, or pursues the ball carrier as a tackler.

The following agility skills help every boy or girl to become a better athlete, and they teach your players to keep their bodies in the proper "ready" position and to be able to move quickly in any direction.

Forward rolls: beginning position. *Landing position.*

Forward Rolls

The youngest children can do forward rolls. Practice of this skill should continue right up through the professional ranks. When correctly done, a forward roll teaches balance, stretches the lower back muscles, and helps to prevent injuries due to falling.

A young child will start a roll this way:

1. Kneel on a carpet, the grass, or a mattress. The mattress is best for safety reasons.
2. Place the hands on the floor with the fingers facing away from the toes.
3. Place the weight on the bottom of the toes. The toes will be facing forward and the heels will be up.
4. Place the back of the head on the floor.
5. Push off with the toes and roll, keeping the legs low.

NOTE: Some children will push the legs up over their heads as if doing a head stand. The legs should not go higher than the hips.

By the time the child is 9 or 10, he should be able to dive and roll. In doing this, he will:

1. Catch the body with the hands (fingers facing forward as explained above).

2. Duck the head as the arms absorb the shock of the fall and lower the body to the ground.
3. Grab the legs with both arms so that the body is in a tight tuck.
4. Keep the head forward as the roll is completed. The head will stay forward until it has moved past the feet.
5. Stand up without pushing off with the hands.

After this diving roll has been mastered, the child can be taught to do a series of three such rolls, coming up and running between each roll.

Shoulder Rolls

Shoulder rolls are more commonly used in football than forward rolls. They should be executed as follows:

1. Players should stand with their feet parallel and wide.
2. Place their right hand near their left knee, palm facing the knee, while twisting the body slightly to the left.
3. Have them bend their knees and place the back of their right hands on the floor.
4. They continue bending their knees while falling forward until they are off-balance.
5. The body's weight will first fall on the back of the right hand or wrist, then on the back of the lower arm, then the back of the right shoulder. As the body continues to fall forward, the weight will be transferred to the back of the head and the back of the right shoulder.
6. The weight will then be transferred across the back from the right shoulder to the left hip.
7. The body will come to rest with the weight on the left thigh and knee.

After the right shoulder roll is mastered, the left shoulder roll can be taught. Then they can be linked, with players executing a right and then a left while coming up and running between each roll.

High knee running

High knee running helps improve the speed of the athlete because it teaches lifting the thigh quickly. One drill to work on high knee running is to have the player running in place for 20 steps and then turn 360 degrees (a full circle) and sprint out.

Running the ropes or running through tires is another way to work on high knee running while combining that running with leg agility.

Coaches once used old tires for players to step into as they travelled the length of the obstacle course. Today, most high school and college teams use "ropes" to run through. A network of ropes about 20 feet long and four or five feet wide is anchored to the ground by four or more posts. The height of the ropes can be from four to 15 inches, depending on the height the coach wants his players to lift their feet. Most are at the 10- to 12-inch level. The professionally designed "ropes" are elastic bands that stretch to the ground if the athlete steps on them. The tires used by players of many years ago could easily cause twisted ankles if players stepped on the tire instead of the ground.

The simplest drill for players when running through tires, inner tubes, or ropes, is to step with the left foot into the first "hole" on the left. They then step into the first hole on the right with the right. He will then continue with the left foot in each left hole and the right in each right hole as he finishes the course.

You can make your own rope course with one-inch PVC pipe. You will need two lengths of pipe about 10- to 20-feet long. (The longer pipes will be needed for older boys.) You will also need two pipes four to five feet wide and enough one- to one-and-a-half foot lengths to be used as supports. This will give you a rectangle which is supported at eight to twelve inches above the ground. String twine or elastic cord between the long lengths of pipe. (For a short course, four supports may be enough. For a longer course, six of eight might by used.) Finally, you will need the offset T's and regular T's needed to connect the frame to the supports.

A better course, which requires more material, is constructed of two full rectangles connected by the supports. This design makes the frame moveable.

After constructing the frame, you will need enough cord (preferably heavy elastic cord) to make squares for your players to run through.

Alternate Stepping

Alternate stepping is done by stepping with the right foot into the left hole then the left foot into the right hole. With this drill, the hips will become more flexible.

If using the ropes, you can have your team practice two-foot jumps. The boy can stay in one line of the ropes jumping forward into two successive holes, then jumping backward one hole, then two forward and one back.

Another pattern would be jumping into the right hole, then the left, then forward, then right, and continuing. Many such combinations are possible.

The football hitting position.

These agility drills not only help to develop coordination, but also speed. They are plyometric exercises. These will be discussed further in the weight training chapter.

Movement in the Football Position

Teaching your players to move in the football position is essential. The football position is similar to most "ready positions" in athletics. Whether the sport is tennis, baseball, defensive basketball, or football, the basics of the ready position are the same. The feet should be spread shoulder width or slightly wider. The knees are bent and the weight is on the balls of the feet. The upper body leans slightly forward, while the arms hang loosely with the hands relaxed. The head is up, and the eyes are forward.

The major difference between the football hitting position and the "ready" position for most sports is that, in football, the back is arched and the head is held higher up. The hands can be in front, as if blocking or playing a hand shiver, or they can be dropped in a relaxed manner and allowed to hang directly down from the shoulders. (Football players will also use the traditional "ready" position when playing running back, linebacker, or defensive back.)

From "the hitting position," players must learn to move sideways and forward with quick short steps, sometimes called chatter steps. The steps should be no longer than six inches. The feet will not come closer than shoulder width, nor wider than six inches outside of the shoulders. As a drill to teach movement in the "hitting position," signal your players to move right or left, forward or backward. The backward movement simulates retreat pass blocking and the forward movement simulates blocking footwork and power running techniques. Always make certain that the proper body position is maintained while they move, and that the elbows are held at a 90-degree angle and pumped as the feet are moved.

The Carrioca

The Carrioca is an agility drill that helps to loosen the hips. In this drill, the player moves sideways by bringing the trailing leg in front of the leading leg, then stepping with the leading leg, then stepping behind with the trailing leg. For instance, if moving to the left, the player brings the right foot forward and one to two feet to the left of the left foot, then steps left with the left foot, then brings the right foot behind the left foot and about a foot or two beyond it, then steps left again with the left foot. This sequence is repeated several times.

The carrioca.

When practicing the Carrioca drill, the shoulders face forward the entire time, the arms are held outward to the side for balance, and the hips move to accommodate and increase the action of the legs.

After moving to the left, the drill should be performed to the right. In moving right, the left foot will be the trailing foot. The player will step with the left foot in front, then behind the leading (right) foot.

Even if your players never excel at football, this step helps them on the dance floor. They can be lovers rather than fighters.

The Three Step Cutting Drill

The three step cutting drill is useful for anyone who runs with the ball. Step at a diagonal (about 30 degrees) to the left with the left foot, step the same direction with the right foot, and then step again with the left foot. On the second step with the left, cut back to the right by stepping at a diagonal (60 degrees) with the right leg. Step in the same direction with the left leg, take another step with the right leg, then cut back to the left.

As players become more adept at making these cuts, they can increase the angle of the cut to as much as 90 degrees and the speed of running and cutting by a significant percentage.

The Three Step and Turn Drill

The three step and turn drill is valuable for any player, but is particularly useful to those involved in a zone pass defense. In this drill, players keep their eyes on an imaginary passer. They start in a parallel stance with their feet pointing at the imaginary passer.

A player's first step will be with the left leg back and away from the passer. The player steps at a 45-degree angle and points the toes in the direction the player will be running. The next step will be with the right leg in the same direction. The player then steps with the left leg and pivots on the toes of the left foot so that the left toes are pointing to the right, at a 45-degree angle from the line of scrimmage. The left foot will have turned three-quarters of a circle. This is not too difficult in a tennis shoe or in a round cleated shoe, but in traditional football or soccer cleats, a player will dig up grass during the pivot.

The Crabbing Position

Moving in the crabbing position (all fours) is important for linemen. Often a block will end with the blocker on all fours trying to maintain contact with the defender. In short yardage and goalline situations, the crabbing position is likely to be necessary for both offensive and defensive linemen.

The proper crabbing position has the feet slightly wider than the shoulders. The weight is divided approximately equally between the hands and the feet. The head is up.

A drill to practice movement in the crabbing position is to have your players move right, left, forward or back on specific hand signals.

IV. Fundamentals of Passing and Catching

Nearly all teams use the pass as an integral part of their offenses. As the pass has become more important, the fundamentals of the passer and the receiver have become more specific and detailed. As a result, there is much more to practice today than a few years ago. As with other fundamentals, skills as common as passing and catching must be practiced correctly every day — even at the professional level.

Passing

Taking the snap is the start of any play. For a T-formation quarterback, the passer's hand should be protected from an errant snap.

The dropback can be either a backpedal or a crossover and run. The quarterback pushes off from the center and steps backward with either foot; most players prefer stepping first with the passing side foot. The quarterback should push off hard with the toes and move back quickly while watching the defensive keys. (A young player might look at just one defensive back to determine if the pass should be made, while a more experienced quarterback might key on two or three players during the dropback.)

The skill of backpedaling is difficult to learn for young players, but it affords the quarterback the opportunity to see the entire defense. It is especially important to use the backpedal drop when a blitz is expected.

Players who use the crossover step while dropping back gain speed while getting to the set-up area, and the technique is easier to learn. But the quarterback sacrifices being able to see the backside defenders because the back is turned. In the crossover drop, the passer steps back with the passing side foot, then crosses over with the other leg and runs back to the passing spot.

Crossover step.

Backpedaling.

Both types of drops should be learned by quarterbacks whose teams use a sophisticated pass offense. It also is good for young players to learn both types of drops so that they will be ready for whatever their high school coaches want them to do.

The set-up spot, the spot from where the pass is thrown, may be one, three, five, seven, or nine yards back, depending on the depth of the pattern. The one-step spot is used on plays such as a quick slant. The three-step play is used in hitches and other patterns that break at about five yards. The five-step drop is used on longer patterns such as those breaking at eight to ten yards. The seven- and nine-step drops are used for long curls and deep patterns.

The coach must select the proper distance for the set-up spot to give the passer a chance to make the proper reads and the receivers time to make their cuts or get to the proper area. All of the set-ups should be practiced.

Quick feet are essential to the elite passer. As the quarterback drops to the set-up spot, stops, and steps up into the pocket, the feet should be in continuous, quick motion. This enables the passer to move quickly to face any receiver who gets open. The quarterback makes the quick move toward the target, then steps with the non-passing leg pointed directly at the target and throws the ball. A common error in hitting a baseball and throwing a football is "stepping in the bucket."

The grip.

This means the quarterback is not stepping directly toward the target and that the hips are open to the target. Incorrect placement of the hips and feet reduces the player's hip rotation, causing a loss of power and accuracy.

The grip should be nearly correct as the ball arrives in the quarterback and from the snap. However, as the passer drops to the set-up spot, the final adjustments should be made.

The size of a player's hands makes a difference in how the ball is gripped. Players with smaller hands must grip the ball a bit farther back to be able to control it and to get the maximum amount of power on the ball without it slipping. (Young players should use smaller balls.)

The most commonly accepted grip is to place the ring finger, the little finger, and sometimes the middle finger on the laces. The index finger is one to two inches from the end of the ball and on the seam. The thumb is two to three-and-a-half inches away from the tip of the ball.

The ball is gripped by the pads on the ends of the fingers and thumb. The palm should not be pressed against the ball, and passers with larger hands may have no contact between the ball and the palm of the hand.

The ball should be carried in both hands at chest height while the passer is dropping back until the passing action starts. The non-passing hand should be lightly touching the far end of the ball. Using

Preparation.

the non-passing hand helps maintain the grip and prevent fumbling. If the passer is hit before releasing the ball, holding the ball with two hands greatly reduces the chance of the ball popping out of the passing hand.

The *throwing action* begins in the same manner as all other hitting and throwing actions. There will be a step and a weight shift, a turning of the hips, and a rotation of the shoulders. The shoulder rotation is followed by the forward movement of the upper arm, an elbow extension, and finally a wrist rotation. All throwing and hitting moves start from the feet and end with the wrist.

The stride forward should be long enough for an effective weight shift forward. Two-and-a-half to three feet is the average stride forward for a college or pro player. A young player's stride should depend on his size. The length of the stride depends on the height of the passer and the distance of the throw. Long passes generally require a longer stride. The toes of the leading foot should point directly at the target. As the stride is starting forward, the throwing arm starts back. The hand should be drawn back close to the head.

The ball should stay close to the ear for most passes. For long throws, the passer may cock the ball farther back. Keeping the ball close to the head rather than dropping it far behind the shoulders, as a baseball pitcher would do, enables a quicker release. The football pass is more like a catcher's throw than a pitcher's throw.

After stepping forward, the passer shifts the weight of the body to the forward foot. While doing so, the hips open toward the target, and then the shoulders rotate into the pass. The muscles of the upper chest are stretched as the shoulders rotate, this gives the upper chest muscles more potential power because the stretch reflex increases their readiness to contract.

From this position, the arm starts forward. The chest muscles bring the upper arm forward. The forearm lags behind the elbow, which stretches the triceps and the muscles in the back of the upper arm. (The stretch enables the muscles to develop more power.)

The player contracts the triceps and the ball starts forward. The speed of the forearm is important in keeping the nose of the ball up, therefore making it easier to catch. The index finger should be the last part of the hand to leave the ball.

If the ball is released too late, it will nose down and fall short of its target. Occasionally this happens to experienced players who are nervous: they hold the ball too long because of their increased muscle tension.

In the follow-through after the release of ball, the palm of the hand should turn down and the fingers should point at the target. After the arm has followed through straight at the target with the palm facing down, the arm can cross the body as it completes its follow-through.

Drills for Passing

The following drills can help young players perfect their passing technique.

1. The passers stand about five yards apart, facing each other. Place both knees on the ground. The coach then checks the following:
   - grip.
   - that the ball is kept near the ear as the pass is made.
   - that the follow-through is straight at the target.
2. Place one knee on the ground—first with the right knee down, then with the left knee down.
3. Drop back to the proper depth (1, 3, 5, 7, 9 steps) and throw at a target.
4. Run in a circle to the right with another player and throw to that player. Check the shoulders being square.
5. Run in a circle to the left with one other receiver.

Passing while running, as in a sprint out or roll out, requires that the passer get the shoulders parallel to the line of scrimmage. The ball should be held in both hands.

Many coaches attempt to get their passers stepping into the pass so that they can use the same action as in a drop-back pass. A passer running right and making a cut on the right foot can pass on the first step (as the left foot lands), the third step, or the fifth step. If running left and cutting on the left foot, the quarterback can pass on his second or fourth step — the steps with the left leg.

Passing while scrambling might not enable the passer to step correctly or even use the proper arm action. It is important, however, to get the shoulders perpendicular to the line of flight of the ball. Without the proper step, the power generated will not be as great. For this reason, the passer should develop strong abdominal, chest, and triceps muscles.

Follow through.

The target varies with the type of pass. It isn't enough to just throw the ball to another player. The pass must be aimed so that it reduces the possibility of an interception. For that reason, shorter passes are generally thrown low. Out patterns are generally thrown low and to the outside. Fade patterns should go over the outside shoulder of the receiver.

Receiving

The effective receiver must know how to get to the proper area, make the catch, prevent the fumble, then run with the ball.

Catching the ball starts with the eyes. The eyes should focus on the ball, even the spin of the ball, so that the player does not lose concentration. It is common for a receiver, especially the less experienced, to take the eyes off the ball at the last second and look for running room. This even happens at the pro level. In order to counter this tendency, players should be coached to watch the ball until it has been tucked safely into the ball-carrying position.

The position of the fingers on the ball depends on where the ball will be caught. The preferable catching position is with the thumbs and forefingers touching or nearly touching. Even a player running deep has a better chance to catch the ball if he turns back towards the passer and uses this hand position.

If the ball is low, such as below the waist, the hands can be held with the thumbs out and the little fingers in. Players running deep and trying to catch an overthrown pass would use this "little fingers in" position.

For a very low ball it is essential to have the elbows together. In this position, it is easier to get under the ball and prevent it from hitting the ground.

Catch the end of the ball. (Some coaches teach to "catch the near stripe.") If the ball is coming fast it often splits the hands and the receiver finishes the catch gripping the middle of the ball. If the receiver tries to catch the ball at or near the middle, it probably will go through the hands.

Cushion the ball as it comes toward the body. Teach your players to reach out for the ball so that they can "give" with it. Keep them watching the ball.

Tuck the ball away into one arm and cup the hand over the end of the ball. Watch the ball into this arm. (Often "overcoaching" a point, such as watching the ball until it is tucked away, pays off with fewer dropped

Overthrown ball.

Low ball.

Very low ball.

balls. By teaching players to watch it past the point where they really need to, players learn to keep their eyes on the ball at least until they have caught it.) After the ball is tucked away, the receiver becomes a runner.

Drills for Receiving

The following drills will improve players' receiving skills.

1. Play catch, with ever-increasing velocity on the passes. Throw high, low, right, left. Check hand positions.
2. The players run toward a passer and catch balls thrown high, low, right, left.
3. The player runs in place and faces away from the passer. The player then turns and looks over his right shoulder and catches soft passes thrown high to the right, low to the right, low to the left (the receiver must turn back toward the passer) and high to the left (the receiver must turn away from the passer, see the ball over the left shoulder, and make the catch).

Repeat the same drills with the player looking over his left shoulder.

Getting off the line of scrimmage is often difficult because the defenders are trying to hit the potential receivers and delay them, thus changing the timing of the play. A wide receiver being hit by a bump and run defender should not allow the defender to push him along the line of scrimmage in either direction. He should work to get directly behind the defender through a fake or a deflection technique.

The simplest fake is the "head bob." This is merely a movement of the head in one direction as the receiver takes his first step straight ahead or in the opposite direction.

A variation of this is the head-and-shoulder fake. In this action the receiver steps one way as he moves toward the defender, then he cuts quickly the other way and gets behind the defender. Sometimes a double fake is needed. If the single fake has worked well, the defender will learn to counter it so the receiver can fake one way, fake the other way, then get behind the defender.

Deflection techniques are used by the receiver who wants to knock the defender's hands away. One method is to rip the closest arm up and through the defender's arms. A player cutting to the right will use the left arm to rip up through the defender's hands.

The "rip-up".

The swim.

The fake block is another deflection technique that is often used by tight ends. The receiver comes out low and makes contact but slides off the defender and continues downfield.

Getting open must be done within the theory of the offense. Some coaches have the receivers run disciplined routes so that the passer knows exactly where they will be as he reads the defense. The design of the pattern should get at least one receiver open. Other coaches want the player to get open in an "ad-lib" manner. By working many hours together with a receiver, the passer can anticipate how the receiver gets open against different types of coverages.

In hook-or-curl passes, the receiver is generally just asked to get between or in front of the defenders in the underneath zones.

Receivers can be taught to read a defender by having a coach or teammate play the role of a defensive back. As the receiver runs at the defender, the defender backpedals. As the receiver gets close to the defender, the defender must turn and run with the receiver. The receiver should watch the defender's feet. When the defender crosses his feet, the receiver should break away from the direction the defender is facing. This technique is very important in getting away from a defender who is playing man-to-man defense, but it also is effective against some zone defenders if they do not keep enough cushion between the receiver and themselves.

Good receivers can set up the defender to break a certain direction, then cut in the direction dictated by the pattern called. If players want to cut to their right, they should move toward their left as they approach the defender then cut back.

Running the route is dependent on the theory of the coach. The traditional way is to run to a point, such as five or ten yards, come under control and make a cut. The cut can be 90 degrees, sharper than 90 degrees (on a sideline pattern), or less than 90 degrees (a post, corner or so on) The player may make a fake before cutting. Of course against a team playing a zone defense, the fake might not be effective.

Players learning these angled cuts should be taught to plant the foot away from the cut, then make the hard cut and accelerate. A player cutting right will plant the left foot. On the more angular cuts, 90 degrees or more, the player must be very much under control, even stopped, when making the cut. The objective is to put distance between the receiver and the defender by getting the defender moving back and then stopping and cutting away.

A second method is to run faster at the defender but run in a slightly S-shaped pattern — a "weave." The receiver tries to get the defender moving back fast and then make a cut.

Getting open against man-to-man coverage is best done by changing directions, (such as a hook and comeback, in and out, hook and go, out and up); getting the defenders legs crossed and then cutting the other direction; getting close to the defender and then leaning into him and breaking the other way.

V. The Quarterback

Offensive backfield drills should be designed to help players make and take the handoff, avoid fumbles, run with power, run with finesse, block, and catch passes. Practices, of course, should be tailored to the individual needs of each position. Fullbacks need work on blocking and power running. Tailbacks should spend time on finesse running, pass catching, and avoiding fumbles. Quarterbacks have other skills they need to develop.

The stance for the T-formation quarterback is to stand very close to the offensive snapper (center). Players should stand as erect as possible, but bend their knees as much as necessary to get their hands low to be in the correct position to take the snap.

The center-quarterback exchange in the T-formation starts with the quarterback placing the passing hand tight into the crotch of the center with the back of the hand providing upward pressure. The other hand faces forward, with the palm and fingers vertical and pointing at the ground. The hands should be at least at a 90-degree angle from each other. A lesser angle may result in the lower hand being hit by the ball on the exchange from the center.

The wrists should touch. It is especially important for younger players to have the wrists touch so that the ball is not driven up between the wrists resulting in a fumbled snap.

Another method of taking the snap has the top hand up, as described above, but the other hand to the side with the thumbs touching.

Whichever method of taking the snap is used, the quarterback must stand as tall as possible to read the defense. He must also give upward pressure with the top hand against the center's crotch so the snapper can feel where the ball should be placed. As the ball is snapped, the quarterback must make certain to "ride" the center with the hands as the center charges forward to make the block. In order to do this, the quarterback must be aligned very tight to the center.

With the wrists touching.

With the thumbs touching.

The next step for the quarterback is to bring the ball into the "third hand," the belly. From this point the quarterback can fake, hand off, or start the dropback.

The quarterback's first step depends on the type of play being run. Some coaches like the quarterback to always use an "open" pivot, opening toward the hole, while others prefer a reverse pivot, turning away from the hole then moving toward it. The open pivot gets the quarterback to the handoff point quicker on wider plays. The reverse pivot hides the ball better from the defense.

In a typical wishbone offense, the fullback runs into the hole so quickly that the quarterback must always open to the hole. The quarterback must be reading the charge of the defensive tackle while reaching back to find the fullback. On the other hand, on a cross buck, the quarterback may be more deceptive by reverse-pivoting (turning away from the hole) then faking or giving to the fullback and halfback as they cross behind.

On a speed option play or the split T dive series, the quarterback may step forward toward the line of scrimmage with the first step. On a freeze option, the quarterback generally will step backward and fake a handoff to the fullback before starting on the option path. On a wishbone triple option series, the quarterback steps back and places the ball into the fullback's gut and rides him, then takes it out and moves forward into the line of scrimmage.

If the play is a pass, the quarterback may step backward with the first step and backpedal to the passing spot. This enables the quarterback to see more of the defense as it adjusts to the passing action. However, it is faster if the quarterback takes a step back with the passing side foot, then crosses over with the other foot, then runs back to the passing spot to set up. In this crossover and run technique the quarterback is looking downfield at the defense, but he won't be able to see the adjustments on the backside very well.

Making the handoff also is determined by the type of offense a team is running. Most teams will have the quarterback hand off with one-hand. Wishbone, belly, and veer teams usually start with a two-handed plant of the ball into the first back running through the line. The quarterback reads the appropriate lineman and decides whether to take the ball back or leave it with the ball carrier.

Most teams use a one-handed give to the runner. Whether a one- or a two-handed give is made, the target should be the stomach of the ball carrier. The quarterback's hand should remain on the ball long enough to make certain there is no fumble on the handoff.

Faking

Faking can be done with one hand empty or with both hands on the ball. The primary type of fake depends on the type of offense a team plays. With teams running a veer or wishbone offense, the quarterback's fakes should be primarily two-handed. Quarterbacks playing in a wing T or I-formation offense use more one-handed fakes.

The quarterback can fake by putting the ball or a hand into the belly of the ball carrier, then taking it back. This is done on cross bucks, belly action, and other plays in which the ball may be faked or given to the first back and then faked or given to the second back.

After making a fake with the ball or the hand, the quarterback can fake with the eyes by watching the player faked to rather than the ball carrier. This is particularly important on play action passes.

The quarterback also can fake by pretending that it is a play action pass and moving deeper into the backfield in a waggle or bootleg action with his hand on his hip, pretending he has the ball.

One-handed lateral pass.

Two-handed lateral pass.

If the quarterback's fakeholds only one defender from pursuit, the fake was effective. If he holds a linebacker in on a play action pass or keeps a defensive back deep when faking a pass on a run play, the quarterback greatly improves his teams chances for success. Most coaches do not work enough on quarterback faking.

For an option type team, such as the wishbone or veer, a quarterback must learn to put the ball into the back's belly and then give it or take it back. The give or take depends on the action of a defensive lineman.

Making the pitch when running an option play against a defensive end is done by keying the end. The quarterback rides the fullback, takes the ball back, then continues toward the defender. If the defender steps away or into the backfield to play the imaginary halfback, the quarterback cuts in. If the defender steps toward the quarterback, the quarterback pitches the ball. A key which is used by many coaches is that if the quarterback can see the numbers on the front of the defensive end's jersey, he makes the pitch, if not, he keeps it and runs upfield.

Some coaches teach the quarterback to make the pitch with one hand, as an end-over-end pitch. Usually this pitch is made "blind," in that the quarterback continues to look at the defensive end. Other coaches teach a basketball type of two-handed pass made while looking at the running back. The blind pass is less likely to be accurate, but the quarterback is less likely to be hurt when being hit by the defender. The two-handed pass is more likely to be accurate, but the quarterback's ribs may be exposed to injury. Rib pads can greatly reduce this possibility.

On a sweep play, the pitch generally is a two-handed toss to the running back. If the play is a quick pitch, it usually is an underhand spiral pass. (A right handed quarterback making a quick pitch to the right will reverse pivot and pass the ball with the right hand. If the quick pitch is to the left, the quarterback opens pivots and makes the lateral underhand spiral pass immediately. Whichever type of pitch is used, it should be aimed slightly ahead of the running back and at chest height.

Drills

The following drills can help the quarterback with the various skills needed to play the position:

1. The quarterback takes the snap and takes the dropback steps necessary for that play, such as an I-formation pitchout or a veer dive.

2. The quarterback drops back with crossover action.
3. The quarterback backpedals while dropping back to pass.
4. The quarterback pitches back to a player starting a sweep.
5. For wishbone teams, the quarterback takes the snap and reaches back for the fullback. If the defending player steps toward the fullback, the quarterback fakes the handoff, keeps the ball, and attacks the defensive end. If the defender steps away, the quarterback hands off to the fullback.

VI. The Running Back

A singular "best" stance for running backs does not exist. The type of stance used must be geared to the offensive theory being implemented and to the individual strengths and weaknesses of the player.

The stance should be determined by the formation, the running back's role in the offense and the quickness of the back . The stance can be a two-, three- or four-point stance, but whatever stance is chosen should be used throughout the season. Changing stances during a game, depending on the assignment, can tip off the defense.

The two-point stance is used by backs who move laterally fast or need to see the defense more effectively. The stance can be nearly upright, as the quarterback or tailback might use. The nearly upright stance enables the running back to see the defense well, but it is not a stance that enables quick starting in any direction. The two-point stance also can be a semi-crouch that enables the player to move forward faster than in the upright stance and be able to move sideways quickly.

In the two-point stance, the weight should be concentrated on the balls of the feet. One way for players to do this is to curl their toes slightly, thus placing their weight forward.

One of the dangers with the two-point stance is that players might get too eager and lean or step before the ball is snapped. This results in a five-yard "backfield in motion" or "illegal motion" penalty. Some coaches have their players take a two-point stance to enhance lateral quickness, but lightly touch one hand to the ground to prevent them from leaning before the snap.

The three-point stance is the most commonly used. The amount of weight on the hand depends on how fast the ball carrier must move forward. If speed to the inside is most important, the inside foot should be back. This would be preferred for a halfback in a belly or crossbuck type of attack. If speed to the outside is most important, the outside foot should be back. If lateral speed in both directions is important, the feet may be parallel or nearly parallel.

Two point stance.

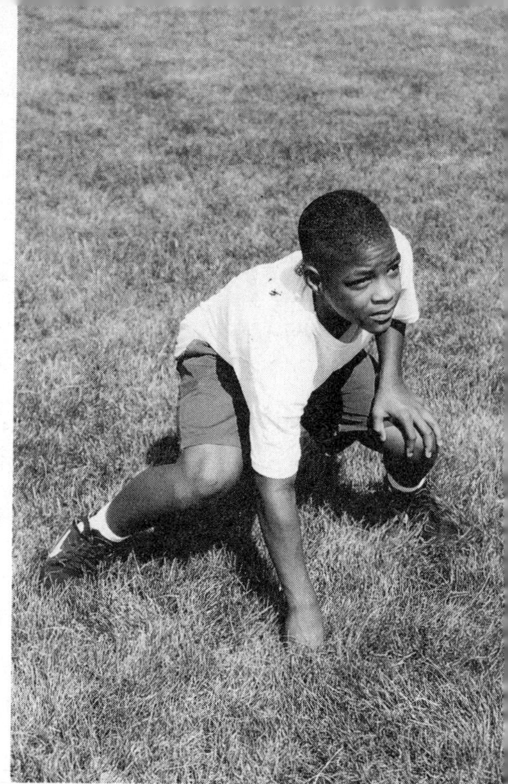

Three point stance.

The four point stance is the least commonly used. It is most likely to be used by fullbacks on wishbone triple option teams, because it helps to get more weight forward which allows hitting the inside holes more quickly.

No matter what stance is selected, the head of the running back must be up and the eyes forward. The back should not look to see where he is going. One of the easiest cues for a defender to spot is the glancing of a back toward his point of attack. He must always look straight ahead.

The start for running backs is the first step or two the back takes after the snap. For a running back, the first step is a lead step (moving the foot closest to the hole first) or a crossover step (the foot farthest from the hole moving first). Some coaches prefer that a running back take his first step as a crossover, others prefer that the first step be a lead step. Some coaches time the back to see which step is more effective for the individual player. In a sweep or a quick pitch action, the type of step isn't really important — whichever step gets the back there quickest is the best step to use.

Some plays, however, require precise timing, so the type of step is of extreme importance. The timing of some plays requires a lead step, while others require a crossover. For example, if the tailback is to take two steps in one direction and then counter the other way, the first step should be a crossover. If the play is starting to the right, the player should step with the left foot, the right foot, and then cut back to the hole after planting the right foot. If the back was to cut after the third step, the player would take a lead step with the right foot, crossover with the left foot, and then step with the right and cut.

Taking the handoff is most commonly done with the running back lifting the inside arm up to shoulder level. The angle of the arm and shoulder and the angle at the elbow should each be 90 degrees. The thumb of the upper hand points down. This helps keep the elbow up

There are two reasons for keeping the arm and elbow in front or inside of the shoulder. First, if the elbow is outside of the line of the shoulder, it can hit the quarterback. Second, if the elbow is wide of the shoulder, the ball carrier cannot clamp down on the ball as easily.

The runner's lower hand should be facing upward and be just past the mid-line of the body. The hand should be held several inches below the navel so that the target area for the quarterback is large.

Taking the handoff.

As he takes the handoff, the runner's eyes should be on the area to which he is running. He should feel the ball as the quarterback puts it into his belly and rides with him. He should then clamp on to the ball with both hands as he heads into the line. It is important to have the ball in both hands because tacklers often rip at the arms and force fumbles.

Running backs can practice handoffs on their own with a parent or friend. They should work from both the halfback and the fullback positions. The player should start running at half speed, looking ahead. After the ball is put in his belly, he clamps down on it. The back should do this while running to his right (left hand up) and then to his left (right hand up).

Catching the pitch is done with two hands. The running back should look the ball into the hands, and then make sure it is in the proper ball carrying position before thinking of dodging tacklers. If the pitch is errant, the running back should fall on the ball rather than try to pick it up and run with it. Pursuing defenders will be trying to pounce on any loose ball, so the back must get to it quickly and save it for his team.

Carrying the ball in the open field is done with one arm. The forward end of the ball can be controlled by placing the index finger over the end, by straddling the end of the ball with the index and middle fingers, or by cupping the ball with the hand.

The runner should feel pressure in three areas: the fingers cupping the front of the ball, the ball on the inside of the elbow, and the elbow against the rib cage.

College and professional players are often seen carrying the ball away from the body and in one hand. This method of ball carrying invites fumbling. Remember that an offensive ball carrier who fumbles and loses the ball has just cost his team a minimum of 35 yards — the yardage the team would have gained on a punt. A fumbled ball is not merely an unlucky "break" or a turnover, it is a major loss of yardage.

Some coaches prefer that the ball always be carried in the right arm. Other coaches prefer the ball to be held in the arm away from the tacklers. (For example, on a sweep left, the ball would be held in the left arm.) Very few coaches advocate changing the ball from hand-to-hand while running.

A ball carrier about to be hit or being hit should again cover the ball with both hands to reduce the chances of fumbling or having the ball knocked away. Defensive coaches often teach their players to rip at the ball as they are tackling the ball carrier.

Players should work hard on avoiding fumbles. They can work on this at home with family and friends. Fumbling creates undue stress on young players and loses ball games. Remember, players should keep firm pressure on the tip of the ball and keep the ball carrying elbow close to the side.

Carrying the ball.

Running back fakes are of two kinds. The first is when the running back is not carrying the ball but has received a fake from the quarterback. The back should cover the imaginary ball with two hands and plow into the line, hoping to freeze the linebacker or be tackled.

The second kind of fake is executed in the open field and involves a change in direction or speed. The most effective fake is for the running back to get the defender moving one way and then to cut behind the defender's back. It helps a great deal if the runner can get the potential tackler to cross his legs. If the defensive player does this, it is a perfect time for the back to make the cut.

The fake can be made with only the head and shoulders or by taking one or two steps in one direction before cutting back. A back can practice cutting by taking three steps in one direction, cutting on the outside leg, then taking three steps in the other direction and cutting again on the outside leg. Continue this three-steps-and-cut action down the field. Start very slowly, increasing speed only when the techniques are mastered.

Another effective fake tactic is changing speed, with the back running either faster or slower. As has been noted, generally the running back runs under control until in the open field. If running under control, the back can speed up just before the tackler prepares to make contact. This hopefully puts the tackler out of position. Changing pace to a slower pace, or stopping, can also throw off the tackler. Slowing down was once a highly effective tactic, but the pursuing defenses of today may catch the back who slows down too much.

A speed fake is most effective when the runner is faster than the defensive back. The speed fake should be done about six yards in front of the defender for an older boy, and three to four yards in front for a boy under age 10 or 11. The back should fake one way and then accelerate in the other direction.

A player can work on this fake with a parent or friend. The player should start running toward the "defender," and then when he is at an appropriate distance, three to six yards, he should kick into a higher gear and outrun the defender, cutting either right or left.

The open field fake is often accompanied by another action to ward off the tackler. The straight arm or stiff arm, the flipper, a lowered shoulder, or a spin can each aid in getting past the tackler or in making a few extra yards.

The stiff arm is an open-handed punch at the opponent's helmet or shoulder pads that is designed to either keep the opponent away from the ball carrier or to push the tackler to the ground. It can be used with either a crossover step or a spin. If the ball carrier is using a left straight arm and is cutting to the right, he should bring the left leg through fast and high while making the cut and drive away from the tackler. If the back is using the left straight arm and wants to cut left, he should spin away by pivoting on the left leg and bringing the right arm and leg away from the tackler. The running back should continue to gain yards while spinning.

Players can practice the stiff arm by holding a stiff pillow, an inner tube inside a gunny sack or pillow case, or a hand shield such as is used by tackle football teams. The players can run at a defender with the ball in one hand and stiff arm the defender with the other hand. The person acting as the defender should sometimes hold the shield high to simulate a high open field tackler while other times holding it low to simulate a diving tackler.

After players learn to make a hard open-handed "punch" at the shield, they should incorporate the crossover step and the spin moves. They should be gaining yardage on these moves. The sequence is to make contact with the hand, execute the avoidance move (spin or crossover), and continue downfield.

The forearm flipper and the shoulder hit are power moves used to get extra yardage through the tackler. The flipper is a forearm rip into the tackler that is designed to push him and possibly loosen his arms from the attempted tackle. The shoulder is used when the ball carrier lowers the body and drives for extra yardage. Each action is more effective if made while cutting behind the tackler.

The stiff arm.

These moves can be practiced with the same type of shield described above, a regulation football dummy or a body bag such as those used in boxing. Those who want to practice these techniques at home might be able to obtain an old bag from a local school coach. If it is cut or ripped, it can be repaired with adhesive tape or sewn with a heavy carpet thread and a curved needle.

In the open field, it is best if the runner can get head up with the defender. This enables him to cut right or left. A runner should attempt to keep the potential tackler set in one spot, then make the defender commit one way with a fake while cutting away from the fake.

Setting up the Block

The runner should use and help his blockers. Experienced runners who are able to outrun their blockers usually slow down and run under control so that the blockers can do their job. The most effective position from which to set up a block is two to three yards behind the blocker.

A simple step to the right forces the tackler to honor the fake and move in that direction. The blocker hits the defend, and the back then cuts left.

Blocking

Backs block with the same techniques as the linemen. The differences are that the backs get to run at their targets so they can deliver more of a blow, but the backs' targets are harder to hit because the defenders have more time and room to maneuver and fake. Also, the defenders are usually bigger than the blocking offensive backs.

Larger backs generally should use the drive block techniques described later. Smaller backs usually should aim lower and use the scramble technique. In blocking for pass protection, they often have to take on a much bigger player who has a run at them. This takes a great deal of courage.

The types of blocks most often used in running plays are the "lead block through the hole" (such as an isolation block) and the "log block." In the log block, a back blocks a wide defender on a sweep by placing his head between the tackler and the runner. He may also use a trap type of block on an off-tackle play, or he may aid a lineman on a double team.

The blocks of the backs are made easier if the coach designs the plays to freeze the defender and if the ball carrier fakes to set up the block.

Preparing for the block.

Pass blocking by a back is similar to that of the linemen. The difference is that the defensive lineman or linebacker has a running start and generally outweighs the offensive back. Because of this, it is essential that the running back sets up properly between the defender and the ball. The back must be ready to pop into the rusher should the rusher attempt to run over him. If the rusher adjusts his path to go around him, the blocker can use his quickness to further redirect the rusher's route.

In preparation for a block, the back's feet should be parallel, the knees bent, the back straight, the head and eyes up, and the hands in front of the jersey with the elbows down.

Power Running

Whether running through the line or driving into a tackler for extra yardage, the ball carrier changes his running style. The legs are widened, with the feet about 24 inches apart or more.) This helps in keeping the ball carrier from being easily knocked off balance when hit from the side.

The ball carrier also must run lower to the ground, with more body weight forward, and be ready to explode into the tackler. Some runners run so low and with so much power that if they are not hit at the line of scrimmage they fall — after gaining about five yards. This is the kind of running needed in short yardage situations.

Running with balance is also important. The effective runner should be able to absorb hits, spin, and cut while maintaining balance. This is another reason that running full speed is not always essential in football. The runner who is hit while running full speed will not have balance. The runner who is under control will be better able to block, fake, and cut. So there is a place for both controlled running and for all-out speed. The effective runner knows when to use each.

An effective drill that develops good balance and effective running skills was devised by former U.S.C. coach John McKay to help O.J. Simpson become a better runner. In this drill, the back "runs the gauntlet" and is hit by players with hand dummies, inner tubes, or pillows. He also can have things such as inner tubes thrown at his feet while others are ripping at his arms to make him fumble or be thrown off-balance.

Drills

1. *Handoff drill, running back to running back.* The ball carriers line up in two lines facing each other. A player in one line carries the ball and runs at a player in the other line, staying to the right. The ball is handed off with the left hand. The receiving player has his inside (left) arm up. The receiving player then carries the ball and hands to the player in the next line. This continues until the coach stops the drill. It is then repeated with the first player running to the left of the player running toward him. The handoff is now made with the right hand and the receiving player again has his near arm (right) up.
2. *Load blocking on dummy.* The offensive back drives at the dummy and blocks, keeping his head on the side opposite the line of scrimmage.
3. *Trap blocking on dummy.* The back runs at the dummy and slides his head to the line of scrimmage side.
4. *Stiff arm and crossover.* The back hits the dummy with the left stiff arm and crosses over with the left leg. Repeat with the right stiff arm and a right cross over.
5. *Stiff arm and spin.* Hit the dummy with the left stiff arm and spin to left. Repeat with the right stiff arm and spin right.
6. *Three steps and cut drill.* The back takes three steps one direction and then cuts, then takes three steps the other way and cuts. The speed and the angle of the cut can be increased as the back gets more proficient at the technique.

VII. Center Snap

The center is the most important lineman on most offensive lines. He should be a leader, and for many teams, he will be the best blocker.

The center's stance utilizes the same principles as the other offensive linemen. If he is to angle block and cup protect, he should be more balanced. If he is going forward most of the time, he should have more weight forward. The center may have only one hand down (the one that's on the ball), or he may have one hand on the ball and the other on the ground for support. This "four-point" center stance is more useful when the center is blocking straight ahead on quick plays.

Starting from a four-point stance, the center lifts one hand (usually the right hand for right-handed players). The ball is placed exactly where that hand had been. The player then places his hand on the ball. This is the position the center takes as soon as the huddle has broken and he has led the team to the line of scrimmage.

Snapping the ball is an extremely important fundamental. The play can't get started if the ball is not snapped properly. The ball can be snapped in different ways. Most teams have the snapper turn the ball as it moves from the ground to the quarterback's hands.

Players can practice the snap by working with their parents, a coach or a friend. The helper should take the position of quarterback behind the player after he has assumed the center's stance. Helpers should start with the ball in their hands exactly as they want to take it — usually with the laces across the fingers of the passing hand. This hand will be firmly in the player's crotch, with the palm down. For a right-handed player it will be the right hand.

From this "perfect" position, the center reaches up and takes the ball from the helper and puts it on the ground. The player should note where the laces are; this is where they should be before the snap. Most right-handed centers will find that they must start with the laces one-eighth to one-fourth of a turn counter-clockwise.

Only the center can be "in" the line of scrimmage. The line of scrimmage is actually a zone bounded by two planes. Each plane extends from each end of the ball, parallel with the goal lines, and as wide as the sidelines. The plane extends from the ground to the sky. Consequently any player, other than the center, who puts the head or an arm into that zone has "encroached" into the line of scrimmage and would be offside if the ball is snapped while in that zone. In high school football, merely putting any part of the body into that zone, even if the ball isn't snapped, is a penalty. This also is "encroachment" and is a five-yard penalty.

When the center comes to the line of scrimmage and assumes the pre-snap stance, the ball should be adjusted so that it is just the way the center wants it for the snap. The center should adjust the ball by placing all five fingers on the near end of the ball and twisting it until the laces are in the desired position. By adjusting the ball this way, the center will not be penalized for attempting to draw the opponents offside with a false snap. This penalty is more likely to be called if the player puts a hand on top of the ball and then twists or moves it.

After the laces are properly positioned, the center should put a hand on the ball and slowly tip it to the desired angle for the snap. The ball should not be moved at this point lest a penalty be called for attempting to draw the opponents offside.

The T-formation snap should be as fast as the snapper can make it. Strong latissimus dorsi and triceps muscles are necessary for a hard snap. The snapper should drive the ball hard up into the quarterback's hands while stepping into his block. It is not "snap, then block" it is "block while snapping." Because the snapper is moving as the ball is snapped, the quarterback must move his hands forward with the snapper until the ball is securely in place. Many fumbles occur because either the snapper slows his arm movement as the ball approaches the quarterback's hands or the quarterback pulls his hands away before he has control of the ball.

The long snap used in single wing offenses and in shotgun attacks is much more difficult to master. In this snap, the positioning of the laces in the pre-snap adjustment should be for the comfort of the snapper. Usually the right-handed snapper turns the laces at least a quarter turn clockwise (to the right), taking a grip as if he were passing the ball.

The snapper can use a one- or two-hand snap. If using a one-hand snap, he merely passes the ball between his legs. If using a two- hand snap, he puts his non-power hand (the left hand for right- handed snappers) on top of the ball. It will be there simply to guide the ball. Using two hands usually is more likely to give a straight pass because the shoulders are forced to stay even. If only one hand is on the ball, the right shoulder may drop and the ball may drift left.

The snapper's stance.

The punter's stance.

Players should learn to look at their target. It generally is best to aim the snap at the thighs or knees rather than at the chest. During the excitement of a game, the snapper is more likely to snap the ball high because he is excited and the adrenaline makes him stronger. A snap aimed at the thighs that goes three feet too high is not a problem. A snap aimed at the shoulders that sails three feet too high may result in a large loss on the play.

The long snap for punting is one of the most important skills in football, and a difficult one to master. Professional teams often draft a lesser player if he is an effective long snapper. A few years ago a Washington Redskins long snapper missed three snaps on Sunday and was cut on Monday. Even the pros have problems with this skill!

The long snapper does not have to be the offensive center. Some teams will use a reserve quarterback or anyone else who can get the job done. The punter might be standing 12 to 15 yards back, so the snapper does not have to block very effectively — but it is essential that the ball be snapped fast and accurately.

The pass can be made directly from the ground or by picking up the ball then snapping it. The snap directly from the ground is the fastest and preferred method.

The snapper's stance should be such that the feet are a good distance from the ball and he can reach out comfortably. By reaching for the ball, the muscles are stretched — and a stretched muscle is more ready to react quickly. The stance should have the feet even, with the toes equidistant from the line of scrimmage. If one foot is back, it may cause the ball to drift to the other side. Most of the weight should be on the balls of the feet. Little weight should be on the football.

The strong arm, generally the right, grips the ball as if a pass is to be thrown. The last two fingers usually grip the laces. The other hand should rest on top of the ball and aid in keeping the ball straight. The ball should be nearly flat on the ground. Lifting the nose of the ball can cause an error in the snap. With both arms moving between the legs, errors that would move the trajectory right or left are minimized. A one-handed snap is more likely to have errors to either side.

The target should be the inside thigh or knee of the punter's kicking leg. The punter should provide a target with his hands, and keep the target low.

The snap count should be up to the center. The punter may yell "set" when everyone is ready. If a defensive team is trying to stunt through the center's area to block the kick, the center should be alerted by a guard. The center can then look around for a possible stunt, prepare for it, then snap the ball.

The snap should be hard at the target. The pre-snap movement of the center's hips should be minimal. Most snappers raise their hips just before starting their backward snapping movement. This upward hip action signals punt blocking teams to start their charge and get a jump on the offense. Players can work on minimizing their hip movement after they have mastered the more basic fundamentals.

As the snap is made, the snapper must watch the target until the ball has left the hands. The palms of the hands should be in an upward motion as the follow-through is completed. The snapper must follow through with both arms, then as the ball is released, snap them forward as the head is quickly lifted upward looking for someone to block.

The center will block passively, as in a pass protection block. After this second responsibility is completed, he can release downfield toward the punt receiver. The other players in the punt coverage wave will set their lanes by where the center is moving.

The field goal and extra point snap must be as fast and accurate as possible. Accuracy, however, is more important than speed. A high, fast snap must be controlled by the holder and then placed down. This takes a great deal of time to learn.

The snap should be low, between one and two feet off the ground. One-foot high is perfect. If possible, the laces should be pointed upward as they hit the holder's hands so that the holder doesn't have to spend a great deal of time spinning the laces forward. The distance from the snapper to the holder is always the same, so an experienced snapper should be able to put the laces where they should be most of the time.

Players should take a normal grip and snap several times, noting where the laces land in the holder's hands. It should be nearly the same each time. Then they should adjust the laces for the center's grip. For example, if the laces continue to be on the bottom when the holder catches it, the ball can be rotated 180 degrees from the previous grip position.

Drills for the Long Snapper

1. Pass the ball overhand (over the head) with both arms.
2. Snap at a target (such as a person, wall, or fence).
3. Snap the ball and quickly assume the blocking position.
4. Snap to a person posing as a punter who is standing five to 12 yards back, depending on the age of the snapper. If the player is five or six years old, the person should stand five to eight feet back. By the time the snapper is 13 or 14, he should be able to snap 12 or 13 yards in the required time.

VIII. Movement and Contact

Football is a game of movement and contact. Every player must be able to move quickly in any direction, and then make contact effectively. These are the fundamental skills of football.

Movement

A football player must be able to move: forward, backward, sideways, on all fours, and in many awkward positions. He must therefore be agile, quick, and at times fast. A player must be able to make contact during movement, and this is learned through proper training.

Simply being big isn't enough. Players who don't move around don't accomplish much more than killing the grass.

Running forward is the basic form of movement. Coaches once told their players to just fall and put their feet in front of them. Today, a great deal of information is available on how to increase a runner's effectiveness.

The mechanics of running require that a player do the following:

- *Run on the toes.* The final power of the pushoff comes from the muscles that extend from the ankle (the calf muscle or gastrocnemius.) By running on the toes, the player's landing is cushioned.
- *Lift the thighs to reach forward and lengthen the stride.* Lifting the thigh quickly forces the hip extensors in the other leg to push backward faster. This is critical in running faster.
- *Push back powerfully with the hip extensors: the gluteal muscles and hamstrings.* This is the primary component of speed.
- *Keep the torso and head slightly forward.*
- *Keep the arms flexed at the elbows at approximately 90 degrees.* The arms should move forward and back, not across the body.

Recommended running techinque.

Young players and their coaches and parents should understand the importance of the cross extensor reflex in running. When the right leg moves forward, the left arm moves forward. By putting extra effort in the swing of the arm, the action of the leg can be increased. This is particularly true when the arm is driven back and aids in forcing the opposite leg backward.

A major weakness in sprinting ability is the slowness of the quadriceps (front of thigh) in pulling the thigh forward quickly. The faster the thigh comes forward, the harder the hamstrings in the other leg can push backward.

The power leg should be "popped backward" (extended quickly) in order to get maximum thrust. The driving leg should straighten. At the end of the pushing phase of the stride, the knee should "punch" forward, not upward. While a longer stride aids in developing speed, it is essential that the feet get off the ground quickly.

A runner should stay low to get started, but should straighten up in order to gain speed. The eyes control the head and the head controls the rest of the body. Keep the eyes forward. This will bring up the head.

Up and down (vertical) movement reduces a person's speed. The runner must strive to be "horizontal" without having the head bobbing up and down. The eyes are a key factor in keeping the head and torso horizontal. If the head moves too far back, the body is forced to become more vertical because the push off from the toes is upward.

The back should be slightly arched. The shoulder blades should be held in and the butt should be under the torso.

The palms of the hands should face inward, not downward. The thumb should lightly touch the forefinger. The elbows should be bent at 90 degrees. As the arms swing up and down, the hands should move from chest to pocket, that is, from chest height (at the top of the forward swing), to the back of the hips (at the end of the backward swing). At the end of the backward arm swing, the wrist should uncock. The runner should feel as if he has a hammer in his hand and snap the hammer at the end of the swing. This extra effort is communicated to the opposite leg which is reaching forward and forces a quicker and farther extension of that leg and a lengthening of the stride, which increases speed.

Running backward (backpedaling) is essential for defensive backs and linebackers and is useful for offensive linemen in pass protection. It also can be used as an exercise for aiding the healing of pulled hamstrings (the muscles in the back of the thigh).

When running backward, the muscles in the front of the thigh and leg supply the power. The upper body must lean slightly forward, the chin should be held down and the arms should be held as they are when running forward.

Backpedaling.

The runner must reach backward with the toe in order to extend the stride as far as possible. Because it is impossible to have a backward stride as long as a forward stride, one's backward steps must be very quick.

The following drills can help young players: running backward for 10 or 20 yards; backpedaling 5 to 10 yards and then breaking to the right or left; backpedaling against a receiver and then breaking with the receiver's cut.

The backpedaling technique can be used in either a zone or a man-to-man defense.

Training for speed is done with quality work. Long runs do not help in the development of speed. Long runs help to develop more of the slow-twitch muscle fibers while speed work and weight lifting help to develop the fast-twitch fibers. Football is not really an endurance activity, so the slow-twitch muscles are not as important as the fast-twitch muscles.

Three types of muscle fibers exist: slow twitch (red), which store hemoglobin and are essential in endurance activities; fast twitch (white), which are used for strength and speed work; and intermediate, which may be trained to become either slow or fast twitch fibers.

To illustrate the importance of these types of fibers to different types of athletes, the percentage of fast-twitch fibers in sprinters is 63 percent, in weight lifters 60 percent, in cyclists 41 percent, and in marathoners 17 percent. Fast-twitch fibers are developed by weight lifting, plyometrics, and sprinting.

The weight training exercises used for speed should be specific. The abdominal muscles, the calves, and the thighs are of primary importance. Shoulder flexors and extensors are also important. One's ability to be strong or fast depends on several factors, as follows:

- *The number of muscle fibers in a muscle that are able to contract at one time.* No one can make all of their muscle fibers contract simultaneously.
- *The number of fast-twitch fibers in the muscle.* An athlete is born with a certain percentage of these, but they also can be developed from the intermediate fibers that are inherited.
- *The strength of the individual muscle fibers.* Strength developing exercises can increase the cross sectional diameter of the muscle fibers, thereby making them stronger.
- The mechanics of the muscle attachment to the bone.

The inherited length of the bones and the placement of the tendon into the bone are very important in developing strength. For example, if two people have forearms that are 12 inches long, and one has a biceps tendon that attaches one-half inch from the joint and the other has a tendon that inserts an inch from the bone, other things being equal, the person with the attachment farther out on the bone will be stronger. For running, if one athlete has a longer heel bone, with the calf muscle therefore attaching farther from the ankle, he will have an advantage over a person with a shorter heel bone.

A highly successful sprint and conditioning program has been developed by Jim Bush, the head track coach at the University of Southern California. He has been the running coach for the Raiders, the Dodgers, U.C.L.A., and U.S.C. In his program, he has the player run 100 yards at about 85 to 90 percent of his maximum speed. The player then jogs back to the starting position. This must all be accomplished within a minute. As the 60-second period ends, the player runs another 100 yards at 85 to 90 percent efficiency. The cycle is repeated 10 times, so it is a 10-minute drill. It emphasizes running fast under control and conditioning.

Coach Bush emphasizes that all-out speed is not generally essential for football players. What is important is how fast they can run while under control. This enables them to cut, spin, and maintain balance: something players cannot do if they are running all out. For this reason, Coach Bush believes that football coaches put too much emphasis on the time for a 40-yard dash and not enough emphasis on controlled running. A football game is not a track meet.

Contact

It is important that youth league players learn the hitting position. The concepts that are helpful in doing so are as follows:

- The legs supply the power. They drive the body through the opponent.
- The back should be slightly arched. The head should be up.
- No matter how high the contact is made, whether at the knees or the chest of an opponent, the tackler's head must be higher than his shoulders, the shoulders higher than the hips, the hips higher than the knees, and the knees higher than the ankles. This enables the hitter to hit up and through the opponent.

When a player hits up and through an opponent, he takes on more of the opponent's weight. This makes the opponent "weigh less" and makes the hitter weight "more." This is because the hitter has more weight on his cleats and the person being hit and lifted has less weight on his feet.

Players should realize that when hitting an opponent, they must be off-balance. If they are well-balanced, they probably will be knocked backward by the impact. A simplified equation shows the importance of this, especially for a smaller player: the weight of the player times the forward speed of the player equals the momentum of the player. Or, *weight x speed = force.*

The weight of the player might change during the hit if the hitter is hitting upward, making himself heavier and his opponent lighter. The forward speed of the player means the speed toward the goalline. If a ball carrier is running parallel to the line of scrimmage and is hit by a player running toward his goalline, the ball carrier has no forward speed because he is not going toward his goal line. If he is moving at a 45-degree angle toward his goal line, such as he might be on a slant play or during a sweep, he would have half of his actual speed credited toward his forward speed. If both players are moving at 45-degree angles, each would have half of their actual speed applied toward the equation.

Sometimes the ball carrier hits lower than the tackler. When this happens, the ball carrier has the advantage and probably will push the tackler backward. However, if the tackler is very big and the ball carrier is very small, the weight advantage in the equation might be such that the tackler wins. If both weigh about the same and the back is moving faster and lower, the back would have a higher moment of "force" in the equation and would win the battle.

Teaching the hitting position can be done anywhere. It might be helpful for players to watch a tape of a perfect professional hit as an example.

When tackling with the wrap-around technique, the arms should be out to the side. When tackling with a lifting technique, the arms close to the body if you want to teach a lifting technique.

Because this is a basic fundamental it should be reviewed every day that you work on football.

Learning to get off balance can be done in a diving drill. This type of drill can be done at home on beds or other soft surfaces at first to learn the proper techniques.

The players should get in a three- or four-point stance. On the command, they dive outward and upward with the head up and above the shoulders, the shoulders above the hips, the hips above the knees, and the knees above the feet. After they have learned how to dive correctly, they can learn how to "dive and drive."

In this drill, one player dives out as in the diving drill, but after extending the legs in the diving action, he drives his legs, taking as many steps as possible before landing on his chest. He should be off-balance throughout the dive and drive action. As proficiency improves, players will be able to take more steps before hitting the ground. Players should stay low throughout the drill, with the head never more than two and-a-half to three feet above the ground.

The legs are crucial to making proper contact. They are the coiled springs that drive the arched backs up and through the opponent.

The "dive and drive" drill is essential to every aspect of contact: the blocker scrambling in a low block, the tackler driving through his opponent, and the runner driving for extra yards. Runners should do the drill with a ball in one arm, covering it with two arms just before contact with the ground.

Learning to get off balance.

IX. Line Stance

Offensive line fundamentals can be taught in many ways. The stance and the types of blocks needed by beginning players depend upon the offensive theory of their coaches. Players in a quick-hitting offense might use a four-point stance and scramble block (blocking on all fours). Players in a run and shoot passing attack would probably use a balanced three-point stance or even a two-point stance.

Stance

The three-point stance is used by most teams. The traditional three-point stance begins with the right toes even with the left instep. The feet are shoulder width apart, or slightly wider, and are perpendicular to the line of scrimmage.

From this basic foot position, players should bend their knees, squat, then align the outside of the right hand just inside the line of the right foot. The hand is placed about 18 inches ahead of the inside edge of the toes for a bigger player and less for a smaller player. The fingers can be extended, with the weight on the pads of the fingers, or can be somewhat flexed so that the weight is carried on the second knuckle and the middle bone of the fingers. The back should be nearly horizontal, with the hips slightly higher than the shoulders, and the head should be up.

Individual differences must be accounted for in determining the width of the feet and the placement of the hands. Shorter players should have their hands closer to their feet. Big players should have their hands farther from their toes. It is the length of the torso that determines where the hand will be most effectively placed.

The other arm will be held below the shoulders with approximately a 90-degree angle of the arm and shoulder and a 90-degree angle at the elbow.

The basic three-point stance.

Adjustments to this basic stance can be made according to the coach's offensive theory. Players on a team that "fires out" hard might want to place their hands farther forward or put more weight on the hand. Players who pull, cross block, trap, or drop back in pass protection usually have a more balanced stance without excessive weight on the hand.

Another adjustment might be the placement of the feet. A team that pulls and angle blocks a great deal might be more effective if the linemen's feet are not staggered; both feet should be equidistant from the line of scrimmage.

Whatever foot position is used, players should remember that it is easier to pull toward the foot that is farther back. So a right guard who generally pulls right would be in a better stance having the right foot back. However, if the guard pulled primarily across the center, he might be better off with the left foot back and the left hand down. If a guard pulls both ways, he might be more effective having both feet nearly even.

The four-point stance (both hands on the ground) is preferred by some coaches. This enables the players to have more weight forward with less discomfort on the hands. Four-point stance teams are usually "quickness teams" that need to explode into the defenders quickly to make a hole for the ball carrier. Some teams will use this stance only in a goal line situation.

Four-point stance.

It is not how far forward the hands are from the feet that enables the player to get off the ball fast. The important part of the stance is how far the shoulders are over the hands. The farther forward the shoulders, the more weight being carried on the hands and the quicker the player can move forward.

Of course the player can't pull or angle block as effectively from the four-point stance, nor can he drop back in cup protection as quickly. Some coaches allow their linemen in a four-point stance to "cheat" by pulling their shoulders farther away from the line of scrimmage if they are pulling or pass protecting. Moving the shoulders back takes more weight off the hands. However, alert defenders at higher levels of play may be able to pick up this key.

Drills

- A player assumes a three-point stance, then fires out on command. The player can do the dive drill from this stance, diving out on his chest. This helps him learn the explosive drive.
- Players can practice the dive and drive drill. From the hitting stance, the player dives out and then drives his legs, pushing him farther forward. Eventually players should be able to take four or five steps before their chests hits the ground. Players should stay totally off-balance while diving and driving.

- From the hitting stance, one player pulls right or left. The player should stay low and throw the arm farthest from the direction he is going quickly toward the hole. This helps bring his shoulders around.

X. Blocking Techniques for Older Players

Players competing at a higher level of Pop Warner or in high school might find some of the techniques discussed in this chapter helpful in becoming a better blocker. The techniques required will depend on the offensive system of their team.

The Start of the Block

The start is the first action from the stance as the player moves into the blocking assignment. Many coaches work on "stance and start" at every practice.

Because the offense knows the snap count, it should be able to get a slight jump on the defense. In fact, well-drilled players can have their bodies six or more inches out of the stance before the defenders react to the movement of the ball or the offensive linemen.

Offensive linemen can be shown the importance of getting the jump with an experiment. Have a player hold his hand wide open with a coin in the palm. Put your hand about 12 inches above the player's hand and tell him to close his hand to protect the coin as soon as he sees your hand start moving downward toward the coin. Unless you are extremely slow, you should be able to grab the coin every time. Obviously, getting the jump is extremely important.

Because offensive players move on sound (snap count) and defenders move on movement, starts should be practiced with the snap count. Offensive linemen should "get off" the ball by anticipating the snap count with the cadence that the team is using.

Blocking

Blocking is the basic offensive fundamental. There are several types of one-on-one blocks, several types of double team blocks, and a wedge block. Two basic blocking techniques are available, the higher

The hand contact block.

targeted drive block and the lower scramble block. These techniques should be used whether the blocker is blocking straight ahead, at an angle, in a double team or combo block, or executing a running trap or a lead block.

The drive block is the most basic block in football. The objective of the drive block is to get the opponent moved away from the line of scrimmage and, hopefully, knocked off his feet. The contact can be made with the heels of the hands or with the shoulder. Some coaches teach the use of the hands for most situations but use the shoulder contact in short-yardage situations. Others use the shoulder block all the time.

The hand contact technique makes it more likely that the defender can be stood up and possibly be pushed onto his back and "de-cleated." It also might enable the blocker to maintain contact with the defender for a longer period of time. It therefore might be more desirable for the teams that allow their backs to "option run" — looking for any hole that develops. This is more common for I-formation teams.

The first step should be with the foot that is farther from the line of scrimmage. The hands, with the fingers pointing upward and the wrists close together, drive under the shoulder pads. This is called "the fit." To learn to keep the wrists close together, young players might want to tie them together with a strong rubber band or string.

The eyes must be under the defender's chest and looking up at his neck. The elbows should be inside the shoulders and pointed toward the ground. The legs supply the power of the block. When the blocker feels that he has the leverage on the defender and is lower, he explodes his legs and arms knocking the defender upward and backward. This should "de-cleat" him and knock him backward. The blocker continues to follow through with his block and finishes the block by landing on the defender.

Players can practice this technique with an old mattress or other soft landing area. Players can be divided into groups of two, with one being the blocker and the other the defender. The blocker makes the proper contact on the partner, then drives the legs until he feels he can lift up and through the defender and knock the defender onto the mattress (de-cleating him) and then falling on the defender. The blocker should hit up, forward, and through the defender. This puts him off-balance forward and gives him the advantage over the defender. The players should then switch roles.

The important points of the hand technique are as follows:

- Aim under the shoulder pads.
- Hit on the sternum with the heels of the hands, fingers pointing up.
- Keep the elbows pointed down and inside the shoulder pads.

- Drive the hands up and through the defender's chest.
- Widen the feet while taking short choppy steps.
- Keep the feet pointed straight ahead.
- Finish the block by continuing to drive, lifting the defender with the arms and legs.
- Drive over the defender, knocking him on his back and then landing on him.

The shoulder contact technique, on the other hand, might be more effective in protecting the hole with the blocker's head. This may be preferable for teams that hit quick and have a designated hole to attack, such as a wishbone or veer team.

In this block, the blocker steps forward with the foot on the same side of the body as the shoulder that will be used to block. This is called the "near" foot. Some coaches want a hard charge directly into the defender; other coaches want the blocker to dip, by dropping the "far" knee, which enables him to hit more on an upward path.

The eyes should aim at the near number of the defender — the number on the side that the blocker's shoulder will contact. It is important that the eyes aim at the body, then have the head slide to the side. If the eyes aim at the side of the defender's body, the point where they will actually finish, the blocker may miss the target completely.

As the contact is made, the blocker should widen his elbow so that the blocking surface is widened. He then lifts and moves the opponent. The lift is made easier by having him "look to the sky" as soon as he has made contact. When the blocker actually looks at the sky he can't help but drop his butt. This gives him a lifting action on the defender.

The blocker also should "pinch with his ear" to aid him in maintaining contact with the defender. Without the blocker's constant attention to applying pressure into the opponent, the opponent may slip off the block. Another aid in reducing the defender's ability to slip the block is to bring the far hand across the blocker's chest and into side of the defender.

The important points of the shoulder block are as follows:

- Aim at the near number.
- Explode into the defender starting with the near foot.
- Extend the blocking surface on contact by widening the forearm.
- Look to the sky.
- Widen the base and keep the feet straight.
- Take short, choppy steps while finishing the block.
- Stop only after you have heard the whistle.

The shoulder contact technique.

The feet should remain parallel with the direction of the block and should widen two-and-a-half to three feet for a high school lineman. Of course it will be less, perhaps two feet, for a normal sized 12 year old. The wider base makes it easier to maintain contact with the defender. If the blocker's feet are too close together, the defender can easily throw the blocker off him.

Keeping the blocker's feet perpendicular to the line of the block is essential for two reasons. First, the action of the hip and knee is more effective if in a straight line. Second, if the feet turn out, a very common mistake, the blocker pushes with the inside edge of his shoe and the few cleats near that inside edge. He has much more traction if all of his cleats are in contact with the ground. This is possible only if the feet are pointing forward. Many coaches emphasize that the blockers turn their feet inward in order to compensate for the natural tendency of most players to "toe out."

The feet should take short, choppy steps. Players taking long steps have only one foot in contact with the ground for a long period of time and could be easily thrown off the defender.

The Scramble Block

The scramble technique is a quicker and lower method of getting to the defender, but the blocker doesn't get the effect of lifting the opponent. The point of aim of the eyes is the lower part of the opponent's thigh.

When scramble blocking, the blocker explodes on the defender using the same technique as described in the "dive and drive" drill. The near shoulder should make contact with the opponent and the opposite hand should be on or near the ground. The player then scrambles while maintaining contact.

The defender might not be contacted effectively because he is slanting away from the block. Because of this, the scramble blocker must always be prepared to use his leg to make the block. If the blocker's head and shoulders have missed the target, he must bring the inside leg up in order to contact the defender. The thigh should be high enough to be parallel with the ground. It should contact the opponent on the thigh.

After the thigh makes contact with the opponent, it drops back toward the ground and the foot returns to the ground. If properly done, the blocker has his near knee between the legs of the opponent and is driving on all fours — "crabbing."

The Uses of the Basic Blocking Techniques

The defender a lineman blocks is not always directly ahead of the blocker. Certain football terms tell the blocker who or how to block. While there may be some small variations in techniques, basically these two above-mentioned fundamentals are used in any of the following situations. Usually, it is up to the lineman to determine which technique he will use. Of course, it is up to the coach to see that he has ample opportunity to practice whichever of these situations he will use in a game.

These basic blocking techniques can be used in many situations in a game. High school coaches teach how to use them in angle blocks, cut-off blocks, hook blocks, reach blocks, scoop blocks, cross blocks and so on. The differences are how the blocker takes the first steps. The principles of the block are the same.

The double team block is basic to power football, and should always create a hole. The two major methods of double teaming are the driving block and the post and pivot.

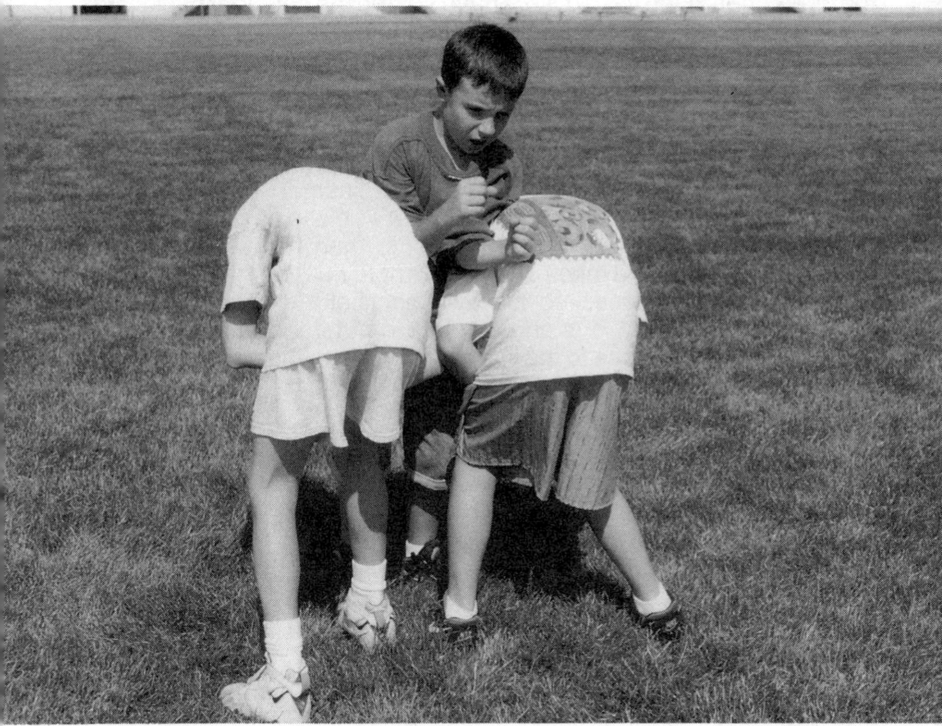

Double team block.

The driving block has both blockers shoulder blocking into the defender. The inside blocker has his head inside the defender and the outside blocker has his head on the outside. This type of block generally drives the defender into the path of pursuing or "shuffling" linebackers, but it may open a hole for a "scraping" backer.

The post and pivot block has the inside man on the double team hitting up and into the defender. This should stand up the opponent. The driving blocker then blocks the defender down the line of scrimmage. This type of block reduces the chance of a scraping or stunting linebacker coming into the hole, but it doesn't cut off the deeper pursuit of other linebackers.

The key point in making any double team block is that the two blockers "seal" their shoulders and hips so that the defender cannot split their block. The defender will try to defeat the double team by either splitting it or dropping to the ground and keeping himself in the hole. The blockers must therefore get under the defender and seal themselves together in order to make the block effective.

Some coaches prefer to teach the double team as merely the start of the block, then when the blockers have started the defender backward, the inside player releases and picks up the defenders in pursuit.

Some coaches prefer to have the outside blocker bump the defender to the far shoulder of the inside blocker then the outside blocker releases on a linebacker.

In the *trap block* the blocker, usually a lineman (most often a guard), passes behind at least one of the other linemen and blocks an opponent. The trapping lineman should get as close as possible to the player blocking the inside of the hole. He then finds the defender outside of the hole and takes an "inside angle out" in which he blocks with the shoulder closest to his own backfield. If the defender is charging aggressively, it is an easy block, but if the defender plays correctly, he will be close to the line of scrimmage and will be reducing the size of the hole so it will be a very difficult block.

Pass Protection

Cup or retreat blocking is done by quickly "setting up." Here, the blocker pops his body into the blocking position while taking a position step to get an inside position on the pass rusher. If the team is using "zone" rules, the blocker sets up ready to take on whomever comes into the area. If the team is using "man" blocking, he takes on a player no matter where that player goes.

The following techniques can be used for the set-up for "man" blocking.

Driving block.

If the rusher is head up, the position step is to the inside with the inside leg. If the rusher is on the outside shoulder, he is already where the blocker wants him so he doesn't need a position step. If the defender is wide to the outside, the blocker steps with the outside foot and quickly slides to a position where his outside foot splits the defender (outside foot in line with the rusher's crotch).

The depth of the set-up depends on the alignment of the potential pass rusher. Many coaches prefer the set-up to be right on the line of scrimmage. Some coaches prefer that the blocker set up a foot or more back from the scrimmage line. The advantage of setting up on the line is that the rusher doesn't have as much area in which to generate speed and to fake. Also by setting up close to the line of scrimmage, the blocker makes the rusher fight for every foot that he gains into the offensive backfield. In addition, a quarterback dropping only three or five steps will have more clear area in front of him. For a quarterback dropping seven or nine steps, the set-up on the line of scrimmage is not as important. Another factor in favor of the quick set-up on the line of scrimmage is that the smaller offensive men will be at more of an advantage starting close to the defender rather than dropping back and letting the larger rusher have a run at him.

If the blocker has to move laterally a step or two in order to get to his assignment, he may have to get some depth in order to be able to meet the rusher. A basic rule for most teams using man blocking in cup pass protection is "big on big and small on small." This means that the offensive linemen will block the defensive linemen and the offensive backs will block the linebackers.

Players also must learn the correct form for pass protection movement. The position of the body in the set-up will be "hips down, head up." The feet should be shoulder width apart and slightly staggered with the inside foot forward. They should be taking continuous quick steps. The weight should be on the balls of the feet. The knees should be flexed and slightly ahead of the toes. The torso should lean slightly forward. (Some coaches prefer the torso to be nearly straight up so that the weight is more balanced. This is more likely to be effective with bigger but slower blockers.) The shoulders should remain square to the line of scrimmage. The head should be up with the eyes looking at the top of the numbers or the lower part of the neck of the pass rusher.

Depending on the rules and a player's experience, the arms may be "locked out" straight or kept close to the body. If they are locked out, they will contact the rusher and maintain contact with him. (While illegal, it is very common for players using this technique to grab the opponent's jersey in order to maintain contact.) With the blocker's arms straight, the rusher has a better chance of grabbing the arms and going over or under them.

If the rusher is trying to grab the blocker, the blocker should counter by hitting the rusher's arm. The blocker must always be prepared to counter whatever moves the rusher is using to attack him.

As the rusher attacks, the blocker must remain between the rusher and the quarterback. The shoulders also must be kept square to the line of scrimmage. If the shoulders are not parallel with the line of scrimmage, the rusher can more easily go behind the blocker's back and get to the passer.

Most of the blocker's hitting action should be up and into the rusher. If the blocker hits out too far, he will be off-balance and can be grabbed and pulled by the rusher.

The feet must move continuously and never cross. Their width should be shoulder width or wider. If the blocker must move laterally, the steps should be short and quick. As the blocker moves laterally, the width of the stance widens six to eight inches and then recovers to the shoulder width starting point.

The following blocking points should be remembered:

- A quick set-up is absolutely essential to effective pass protection.
- The feet should be shoulder width apart and always moving.
- The feet must be pointed straight ahead.
- Get position inside the rusher. Always protect the inside.
- The knees should be flexed and slightly forward of the toes.
- Keep the head up and the eyes looking at the top of the numbers.
- The shoulders are always parallel with the line of scrimmage.
- Punch the arms up and into the numbers of the rusher.
- Let the opponent come to you.
- Honor inside fakes, but ignore outside fakes.
- Keep the rusher's hands away from you.
- Pop up at the rusher, not out.
- Give ground slowly.
- Remain up and balanced. Only if beaten will the blocker try to cut the rusher with a low block.
- After the pass is thrown, cover in case the ball is intercepted.

XI. Tackling and Ball Stripping

Tackling is the basic defensive fundamental. While defensive linemen often tackle by simply reaching out and grabbing the ball carrier, they should be taught the basic fundamentals of perfect form tackling.

The ideal tackle is made with the head up, back arched, legs driving the back through the ball carrier, the arms wrapped hard around the ball carrier, the eyes open, and the ball carrier being driven backward.

High form tackling teaches the defender to hit with the legs, keep the back arched, keep the eyes open, and wrap the arms. In teaching this technique, the ball carrier moves into the standing tackler who is in the form tackling position (back arched, feet wide, and arms out to the side. When the ball carrier is six to twelve inches from the defensive player, he explodes his legs, aims his nose about four inches from the side of the ball carrier, makes contact, extends up and through the ball carrier, and wraps his arms around the offensive man keeping the arms parallel to the ground. (Players tend to drop their arms lower than the shoulder level. This humps the back, which places more strain on the lower back muscles and reduces the upward lift.) The defensive player carries the ball carrier five or six steps. His arms must be wrapped hard or he will drop the offensive man. Obviously the players should be about the same size.

Some coaches prefer another arm technique. Rather than having the arms to the side to wrap around the runner, they prefer that the arms stay close to the body and then drive up along the sides of the ball carrier. It is haped that this will cause a fumble.

The following are important points to remember in high form tackling:

- The defensive player's back is arched back, not humped forward.
- The eyes stay open through the tackle (the eyes should "explode" open as the legs "explode" upward.)
- The arms are parallel with the ground.
- The legs maintain a wide base throughout the tackle; players can practice with a partner and lift each other with leg power.

The high form tackle.

This skill should be taught moving forward into the tackle, alternating hitting with the right shoulder and then the left shoulder. It should then be taught moving diagonally into the ball carrier with the right shoulder and then the left shoulder, keeping the head in front of the ball carrier.

This skill is seldom used in a game, but it should be learned because it emphasizes all of the basic fundamentals of tackling. When used in a game, it generally is in the kicking game or when a linebacker steps into a hole with only a ball carrier coming at him.

The low form tackle is more common. The fundamentals remain the same as in the high form tackle, but the tackler is off-balance and lower as contact is made. His base is wide. His head is up, and his back is arched. He explodes through the ball carrier as he drives his legs. He finishes with his body on top of the ball carrier's and his arms wrapped around the player.

It is essential that the tackler learns to get off-balance as he explodes. This is true whether he is hitting directly into the ball carrier or attacking from the side. Injuries can occur when this technique is practiced, so it might be wise to practice these tackles onto a foam high jump pit or an old mattress to cushion the blow.

The low form tackle.

Stripping the ball is seen more and more at the professional level, but it is not used enough at the lower levels. Remember that if a ball is stripped from the offense and recovered by the defense, it is worth at least the distance of a punt. So a stripped ball fumble would be worth at least 25 yards -- three-and-a-half first downs.

Players can learn how to strip the ball by lifting outward on the ball carrier's elbow with one hand, then punching the ball past the elbow with the palm of the other hand.

Professional players often grab the ball or the ball carrying arm and pull it downward. This technique is especially effective against the players who do not carry the ball properly -- carrying it at arm's length rather than in the crook of the elbow.

Ball Stripping Drills

- Have someone hold the ball in one arm while the players, one-at-a-time, lift that person's elbow with one hand and punch the ball with the other hand, which is open.
- Someone carries the ball in one arm and a player comes from behind and to the side and rips downward at the ball carrying arm while making the tackle.

Stripping the ball.

XII. Defensive Line Fundamentals

Many coaches believe that defense is the most important part of football, and defensive play starts with the play of the line. It is at the line that the team has the first opportunity to stop the run and the pass. Defensive linemen must have great physical courage.

As with the offensive line, stance, charge, and reaction are important to the defensive line. However, while the offensive blocker knows where the play is going and how he will block for it, the defensive lineman must neutralize the blocker, react to keys that the offense gives him, pursue the ball, and make the tackle.

This chapter gets a bit technical. Beginning players cannot be expected to understand everything the first season. Coaches should focus only on what is necessary. For example, a team that seldom encounters a double team block need not work against it. But all defensive linemen will be called upon to rush the passer, so this skill can be practiced by all, despite age or level of experience.

In the past, the defenders' primary advantage was that they could use their arms. This advantage has been reduced because blockers can now use their hands.

The stance for a defensive lineman generally has more weight forward than the offensive lineman's stance. This is because a good offensive lineman will have moved about six inches before the defensive lineman can begin to react. By having more weight forward, the defender is better able to equalize the momentum of the offensive player.

The defensive stance can be a three- or a four-point stance. If the player's stance has a great deal of weight forward, the four-point stance may be more comfortable.

Players who do a great deal of slanting and looping (defensive lateral movements) might use stances that do not have as much weight forward as would the players who are hitting directly into the blockers, therefore the type of stance is often adjusted depending on the defensive theory of the team or the assignment for that particular play.

If forward momentum is important, such as in a pass rush, the feet should be staggered. If lateral movement is important, such as in a looping charge, the feet should be parallel.

The back should be straight. The hips can be higher than the shoulders. The shoulders should be even. The head should be up. The eyes should be focused on the man ahead.

The alignment will generally be head up, inside or outside shoulder, or in the gap. If the lineman's responsibility is to penetrate the gap, he may play very close to the line of scrimmage. If he has to control a man and two gaps and is often being defeated by the player or players in front of him, he may back off the line to give himself more time to read and adjust to the block.

Pre-snap cues may help the defender to make an educated guess as to where the ball will go. Prior to the snap, he can glance at the position of the backs. Have they "cheated" into a position that indicates a special play will be run? Is a back wider? If so, his position may signal a quick pitch. Has the back cheated up? He may be preparing for a dive or trap.

A defender can also look at the eyes of the backs. Often backs will look at the area they are going to attack, either as a ball carrier or blocker. This is particularly true for players at the lower levels, up to high school play. The blocker in front of him may be peeking laterally, possibly signalling a cross block or pull. He also may be leaning in the direction of the pull. He may have more weight forward than normal. Less weight on the hands may signal a pull or a pass block.

You should encourage your players to spot these tips after they have learned the basic movements. For the younger players, however, just working on the stance, charge, and the work of the hands in warding off the blocker or getting past the blocker in a pass rush may be confusing enough.

The charge begins on the movement of the ball (the snap) or the movement of the offensive player. Both of these should occur at the same time. The target of the charge can either be a man or a gap. If charging into a man, the blocker must be neutralized. If charging into a gap, the defender must avoid the blocker.

The charge must be low. Remember that the lowest man nearly always wins in football. The defensive lineman must hit hard enough with his legs to be able to stop the offensive blocker's charge. He must also get under the offensive blocker and lift him.

The defender's initial charge will be with leg power, with the back arched slightly, and the head up. Defenders are allowed to use their hands and arms more than are the offensive blockers. This makes it easier for the defender to ward off the block and get under the blocker.

Block protection is the term used to denote the type of hand or arm action used to ward off and control the blocker. There are several types of block protection, with varying terminology. The choice of technique depends on a player's build and the assignment. A shorter player probably can get under a taller player with a hand shiver. Any player can use the forearm rip or other techniques, as follows.

The hand shiver (jam or forearm shiver) is the most common use of the hands. In the hand shiver, the defender hits up and into the offensive blocker. He drives his hands into the blocker's chest or the lower part of the shoulder pads and lifts the blocker upward as he charges.

The arms should "lock out," keeping the blocker at arm's length. The elbows should be under the shoulders as they start their lift. If the elbows are wide, the blocker's legs can overpower the defender's arms and the blocker has a better chance to get into the defender's body. If the defender makes the arm movement with his elbows down, even if he can't lock out his arms, he will have his forearms between himself and the blocker.

The arm lift is a one-handed shiver used primarily when the defender is protecting a gap different from where he lined up, such as controlling the outside gap from an inside shoulder alignment. The player steps with the foot farthest from the direction he is moving (the "far" leg) and hits upward with the "far" hand lifting under the pads, as in the two-hand shiver. The near hand is then free to play the outside of the blocker. So, if moving to the right, the defender would step laterally with the left foot, hit with the left hand, then keep the outside leverage with the right arm and hand.

The forearm rip (forearm lift or forearm flipper) is a second type of shiver. In this movement, the defender makes a hard charge with his shoulder into the blocker. As he makes his shoulder hit, he lifts his arm up and through the blocker. The arm should have a 90-degree angle at the shoulder and elbow. The power comes from the shoulder muscles (deltoids). As the forearm hits under the pads of the blocker, the defender's back arches more, the hips drop, and the legs assist in the lift. By this time the blocker must be defeated.

The hand shiver.

The forearm rip is not as effective as it used to be because blockers can now use their hands. It is more difficult to get close enough to the blocker's body to rip into it. On the other hand, the forearm rip can get the blockers hands off the defender's body and the defender will still have one arm free. This technique can therefore be used in a gap control defense or when slanting or looping.

After the blocker is defeated, the defender carries out his assignment. Most teams today use a "gap responsibility," meaning that the defender neutralizes his man and then protects a gap. After it is certain that the defender's gap is not the hole which the offense is attacking, he can pursue the ball.

A shiver drill can be executed into a bag, an arm shield, or a sled. The players explode their bodies, make the desired shiver (hand or forearm), then drive their legs. In the beginning, this skill may be done with the defender on his knees popping his shiver into a blocking bag. Technique should be emphasized: elbows and shoulders at a 90-degree angle for the forearm shiver; elbows in and down for the hand shiver.

The butt and control (or blast and grab) is used against blockers who aim high. The defender drives his face into the blocker's chest with his hands hitting near the low part of the blocker's numbers. He grabs the opponent's jersey and hand shivers him as he neutralizes his charge and fights the pressure. This technique enables the defender to get a great deal of power from his body. He then fights the pressure and disengages.

Varying the Charge

The defensive lineman might not always want to hit the offensive lineman in front of him. He might angle into a gap or hit an adjacent man rather than the one he was lined up against.

The slant charge is a direct charge at an angle from an alignment on a man to an adjacent gap (a penetrating charge) or into the next offensive man (a controlling charge). If it is into the gap, the more common slant, he should align on the line of scrimmage. He steps diagonally with the far foot (the left foot if going right) and then with the near foot. He protects himself from the nearest blocker with the far hand, the hand that was farthest from the blocker when he started his charge, as he charges into the gap. He aims at the near hip of the adjacent offensive lineman.

The slant charge.

Some coaches use a slant into an adjacent man. This may be done from a gap alignment or from a position about a foot off the line of scrimmage. The charge is the same except that the target of the charge is the near shoulder of the adjacent man. He shivers that man, usually with a hand shiver, and reacts to the pressure.

The loop charge is made around the adjacent man. It may be from an inside position on a man, around his head and into a gap that he will penetrate. It can also be made from the adjacent man to the next man on the line of scrimmage, in or out. If looping, the defender needs more distance from the line of scrimmage, as much as a yard, depending on the width of the line splits and the abilities of the blockers.

The charge is started with the far foot stepping laterally, then the near foot. The far hand must offer block protection. If the target is the gap, the defender will penetrate. If it is the adjacent man, he will hit and react to the pressure.

The goal line charge starts with a stance that has the feet close to the line of scrimmage and a great deal of weight on the hands. On the snap, the defender dives through his man or through his gap at about knee height. He then brings his legs up quickly and continues his penetration into the backfield.

Reading the first step of the blocker can assist the defender in knowing how to make the initial charge. Many coaches teach their blockers to step with the foot on the same side as the shoulder with which they will hit. This gives the defender a jump on his reaction. He can start his lateral movement before seeing which way the blocker's head moves.

If the blocker pulls, the defender can be taught to follow the pull. However if a team uses the "influence trap," the defender must be aware that a trapper may be coming from the other side and block him from behind. This is more likely to occur if his man pulls outside and a guard from the opposite side of the center traps him.

If his man blocks the next man in or out, the defender should have hit him to slow the blocker's charge. He can expect a similar block or trap to be set for him. If he is blocked by an adjacent man, he must fight the pressure, but he must also expect a trap. In organized football, the scouting report can give him an idea as to what type of blocking scheme he must counter. Most traps will come from the center out but some teams now trap from the outside in.

Playing the angle block can be expected if the offensive man lined up on the defender blocks the next man to either side of him. If the man on him blocks to the defensive right, he can expect a blocker coming from the left, a cross block coming at him from the right, a trap block from the right, or a lead block from a back. The defender must fight the pressure of the blocker and not be driven off the line of scrimmage.

The first move should be made into the blocker to keep him off his assignment. This does two things: it helps the defender regain his balance while he recognizes who will be attacking him and it slows the blocker who had aligned in front of him and reduces the blocker's effectiveness in blocking another defender. After seeing or feeling the man who is attacking him, the defender should hit him with a forearm rip with the arm nearest the blocker. He should then work to control him and fight the pressure with his far hand and his legs. If all else fails, he should drop to all fours to create a pileup at the line of scrimmage.

The trap block is another possibility. If the blocker on the defender blocks down on the next man and the defender feels no pressure, he probably is being set up for a trap block. The defender should then narrow the gap between himself and the blocker who is blocking down the line. He should not move across the scrimmage line, but should set for the trap and get ready to play it with the outside arm, with a forearm flipper, or the hands. Some coaches teach their players to drop to the inside knee when they feel no pressure. This puts the defender lower than the trap blocker and can reduce the trapper's effectiveness.

Seeing the near back's first step may also give a hint of the type of play being run. Is he coming right at the defender as a blocker or a ball carrier? Is he moving across the center, indicating that the play will not come quickly at the defender?

On a pass play, the defender should check on the first step of the near back. If the near back steps out, the play probably is a pass block. However if the fullback stays in one spot or a halfback steps inward, it probably is a draw play.

Protecting the Gap

Responsibility is essential for teams that play gap control defenses. If playing gap control, the defender hits into the blocker with his head and shoulders and then slides his head to the side of the gap that he is controlling. While doing this, he hits upward with the hands in a hand shiver, stops the offensive charge, then separates from the blocker. The defender's feet must keep moving while the legs provide upward and forward pressure on the blocker.

Fighting the pressure is the next job of the defender. If the defense is playing a "hit and react" technique, the defender "reads the head" of the blocker. This means that he is aware that the blocker is trying to take him one way, opposite the blocker's head, so he fights through his head. The defender should never go around behind the blocker. He should always cross the face of the blocker and move to where the ball carrier probably will run.

The loop charge.

The goal line charge.

To practice this technique, a player can put his head on one side of the defender. The defender then shivers the blocker and moves across the blocker's face. As the defender gets better, he can start to move his feet as he sees the blocker's head moving in one direction. If a blocking bag or shield is available, it can be pushed at the defender to one side and the defender can shiver the blocker and move across it.

As he reacts to the pressure of the block, the defender must never cross his legs as he moves toward the ball. His feet must be wide so that he has lateral balance. His legs should move quickly and take short choppy steps.

If the blocker drops back in pass protection, this signals the defender to attack the blocker. The defender must attempt to turn the blockers' shoulders and take the proper pass rush lane. In this reaction, the defender should use the hands, not the forearms, because using the arms gives him more ability to maneuver and whip the blocker.

Linemen can practice these skills by working against a teammate or coach who sets up as if in pass protection. The defender hits the offensive lineman with his hands on the lineman's chest and then starts to move one way or the other while attempting to get the offensive player to turn his shoulders.

Fighting the double team block can be done a couple of ways. The defender can choose to whip one blocker. He can drop to the ground, reducing the effectiveness of the block. He can split the block, or, if defeated in attempting to overpower the block, he can spin out of it.

This spin can also be used against single blockers who have made effective shoulder blocks from straight on or have had an angle on the defender and are blocking down on him. Remember, the spin should be a last resort because the defender will have his back to the ball for an instant. Also, if the defender spins as his first reaction the blocker may "false block" him -- hit him on one side (the side away from the direction he wants him to move) and let the defender spin himself out of the hole.

Pursuit

Pursuit to the ball is the next job of the defender. If the defender is not directly attacked, he must quickly discover where the ball is going. He must then take a path that enables him to intercept the ball. If it is a pass, the rusher follows the ball and gets to where he can make the tackle if the receiver is delayed or runs laterally.

In taking a pursuit path, a cardinal rule is to "never follow your own color." Every defender must be taking a route that gets him to the ball carrier without having to run over his own man.

Trailing the play is the responsibility of one of the defensive linemen -- usually the widest man away from the play. He should be alert to counters, reverses, bootlegs, play action passes, and cutbacks. His path should be as deep as the deepest man.

XIII. Pass Rush Fundamentals

Pass rush fundamentals are easily practiced at home. Most lower level teams, such as in Pop Warner and high school, concentrate on teaching more basic skills, and the players often are not able to practice these techniques. At the pro level, where the players are specialists, defenders might have 20 to 30 minutes a day to work on pass rush techniques.

Young players can enlist the help of their family or friends to work on these techniques. Coaches can designate one practice each season for family members or friends to come learn drills that can be practiced at home.

The stance was described in the chapter on defending the run. After players have learned the stance, they know that their primary responsibility in rushing the pass is to put as much weight forward as possible.

The pass rush begins with the defender's recognition of a pass play. The backward, non-aggressive steps of the blocker in a drop back pass might be the tipoff. Play action passes take longer to recognize because the blocking is more aggressive. Once recognized, the defender should yell "pass" to alert his teammates.

The defender should already have started his rush by getting his hands on his opponent's jersey at chest to shoulder level. He must charge hard to defeat the blocker. Several techniques can be used, depending on what the blocker is doing.

At the higher levels of play, either scouting reports, films, or a few minutes of playing against an opponent should tell the pass rusher how the man in front of him is blocking and what his weaknesses are. Remember, football is a game of head, heart, and body. Thinking effectively makes for better players.

Does the blocker have too much weight forward or backward? Can his shoulders be turned? Are his feet quick enough to stay with the rusher? Does he have a weakness that can be exploited? Players can learn a great deal by watching games on television and looking for the weaknesses of various blockers.

After the play starts and the rusher has his hands on the blocker, he can try to charge through the blocker or attack one side. A big defensive end attacking a smaller offensive lineman or a back may decide to run right through the blocker. If the blocker is retreating fast and has too much weight on his heels, or has excessive momentum backwards, he may also be susceptible to a head-on attack.

If the match-up is even, it is better to attack one side of the blocker. Whatever the blocker's technique and size, there is a pass rush technique to beat him.

Basic Pass Rush Techniques

The bull rush is used against a fast retreating blocker whose weight is on his heels. It also can be used by a big strong defender against a smaller blocker. In this rush, the defender rushes hard at the blocker, punches the heels of his hands into the outside of the chest or under the armpits of the blocker, and drives his legs hard as he pushes the blocker into the passer. Because the defender is the aggressor, he may be able to knock down the blocker. Linemen or big backers being blocked by smaller backs often use this type of rush to intimidate the blocker.

The jerk is used against a blocker who has too much weight forward. The defender should start the charge forward and then, as the blocker lunges forward, grab the blocker's jersey or pads and pull him forward as he goes around him.

Rushing One Side of the Blocker

Most pass rushes will be to the side of the blocker. The defender should get the blocker's shoulders turned away from the line of scrimmage. As he does this, he can attack with power through that shoulder. Following are some techniques to attack through the shoulder that is turning away from the line of scrimmage.

In the *rip and run* technique, the defender drives his far arm with a hard rip under the near arm of the blocker. So if the defender is going to the right (the left side of the blocker), he hooks his left arm under the left shoulder of the blocker. As he hooks the shoulder of the blocker,

The bull rush.

the defender lifts up on the shoulder as he charges. This technique eliminates the hands of the blocker as weapons, turns the blocker's shoulders, and eliminates the blocker's ability to cut him as he moves past him.

The wrist club and swim is another technique used to the side of the defender's initial charge. The defender steps with the far foot and moves to the side of the blocker. When he is close to the blocker, he grabs the hand or forearm of the blocker or hits it with his forearm. This action knocks the blocker's arm off the rusher and creates a path for the rusher. Then he swings his far arm over the near shoulder of the blocker in a swim-like move. If he is going to his right, the rusher steps with his left leg as he moves toward the blocker's left side. He uses his right arm or hand to hit the left arm of the blocker. He then brings his left arm over the left shoulder of the blocker in a "swim" move as he moves past the blocker.

The shoulder club and slip has the rusher hit the blocker with a hard blow of his hand into the shoulder pad or upper arm of the blocker. The shoulder of the blocker should be lifted in either case. The rusher then drives his far shoulder under the armpit of the blocker. This is a good technique for shorter players working against taller blockers. In this case, the rusher can grab the area near the elbow of the blocker and lift as he charges under the arm. If going to his right, he hits the blocker's left shoulder or arm upward with his own right hand, then drives his left shoulder under the left shoulder of the blocker. The legs must continue to drive through the entire action.

The bull rush and slip is slightly different. The defender starts forward in the bull rush technique, but as the charge continues the defender lifts one shoulder of the blocker and then brings his far arm under the blocker's shoulder and drives past him.

If moving to the right, the defender starts with both hands on the chest of the blocker while driving him backward. Then, if he can lift the blocker's left shoulder, he drives his own left shoulder and arm under the blocker's shoulder and slips past him. This technique is often seen in professional games.

Reversing the Rush

Another method of pass rushing is to start the blocker's shoulders turning one way and then attack the other way. This should be done only after the blocker has overcompensated for the outside rush and is somewhat off-balance.

The pull and swim technique has the defender start in a hard rush to one side with his hands on the chest of the blocker. As the blocker turns his shoulders in one direction, the rusher either grabs the jersey or

The wrist club and swim.

reaches behind the shoulder of the blocker and turns the close shoulder (the shoulder closest to the line of scrimmage) toward him as he swims over it with the other arm. If the rusher is charging to the right and the blocker's shoulders turn in that direction, the defender grabs the blocker with his left hand pulling the blocker's right shoulder toward him as he swims his right arm over the blocker's right shoulder. This works well for taller defenders.

The reverse club and slip is used by shorter players. They start the rush to one side while turning the shoulders of the blocker in that direction. As the shoulders turn, the defender reaches up with his trailing hand and grabs the elbow or upper arm of the blocker, pushing it upward and then ducking under it by driving his far arm under the blocker's upraised arm.

If starting to the right, the hands would be on the blocker's chest. As the defender charges hard to the right, he works to turn the blocker's shoulders with him. As the blocker's shoulders turn, the defender releases his left arm from the blocker's chest and drives it under the blocker's right arm, punching it upward. He then reverses his direction and ducks under the blocker's right arm pit.

The club and spin is another technique to reverse the charge of the rusher. The rusher starts his normal rush, as above, but with the pressure to the outside of the blocker. The rusher hits hard into the midsection of the blocker with a hand or forearm and whips his other arm behind him, spinning to the inside. The spin must bring him closer to the quarterback, not back to the line of scrimmage or parallel with it.

If the rusher is starting to the right, he attacks the left side of the blocker with both hands on the blocker's chest. As the blocker compensates for the outside rush, the rusher pushes hard with his right hand and then whips the right arm behind him spinning to his right. He steps back with his right leg, pivots, follows with the left leg as he gains ground toward the passer, then finishes with the right leg stepping toward the passer. The left arm pushes and releases during this spin.

The arm lift and charge is perhaps the most effective pass rush technique, but very few players have the strength and skill to use it. In this technique, the rusher grabs the wrist of the blocker with one hand and then raises it over the head of the blocker. He hits the blocker's chest with the other hand and raises him as he charges directly through the blocker.

For example, the rusher can grab the left wrist of the blocker with his own right hand. He lifts the blocker's arm straight up and over the head of the blocker, putting the blocker off-balance. He hits the blocker's chest with his left hand as he drives through the blocker.

Stopping the draw play can be aided if the rusher is aware of the steps of the potential runner. If he sees the back step out wide, he can assume that he will become a blocker or receiver. If the back stays in the same spot or steps inward, he probably will run a draw.

Players can work with family members or friends in developing some of these techniques. They might want to work on only one or two; it is better to know one or two skills perfectly than to know several but be inefficient at making them work.

XIV. Inside Linebacker Play Against the Run

Linebackers are the backbone of the defensive team. They must be sure tacklers and they must be prime run defenders, but they are also prime pass defenders. Offensive strategies and tactics are often devised to fool the linebackers. Faking the run and throwing the short pass, faking the dropback pass and running the draw, starting the play one way then countering opposite — all are ways of fooling the linebackers.

Linebackers must learn to be disciplined in their responsibilities, but they should not be robots. They should be able to play recklessly within the scope of their assignments. They cannot prepare for every situation they will face, but they can learn to recognize their responsibilities.

Inside Linebackers

The stance for linebackers is a two-point stance. Inside backers can be more upright because they will be farther from the blockers. The toes are parallel to the line of scrimmage and the feet are one to two feet apart, depending on the player's size. The knees should be flexed. The torso is flexed forward, and the head is up. The hands are at about chest height if a blocker is an immediate threat. If the blocker is one-and-a-half yards or more away, the arms can be dropped comfortably in front of the body. The weight should be on the balls of the feet.

Movement of the linebackers is primarily lateral while they are in the hitting position. The backer should shuffle sideways (not crossing the feet) while keeping the shoulders parallel to the line of scrimmage. It is only as a last resort that the backer turns and runs. Plays such as a quick pitch or a spot pass to a wide receiver would be last-resort situations.

A simple drill for linebackers is to assume the hitting position and move sideways on a signal, never crossing their feet. When they can do this, they can learn to move forward into the hole when the ball moves towards it. As the ball carrier moves sideways, the linebackers (one-at-a-time) also move laterally, staying about a yard behind the ball carrier and moving their feet quickly (chatter stepping). After the ball carrier breaks into the hole, the linebacker attacks the carrier through that hole, making certain not to overrun the ball carrier.

Keys for inside backers are tipoffs given by offensive players that indicate what the play is going to be. Linebackers may key on a lineman or a back. In some cases, they can key the spin of the quarterback. If the basic plays (not the counters) always go to the side toward which the quarterback opens, the linebacker can start in that direction. Some teams always reverse pivot so the backer can start to the side away from which the quarterback turned. Most teams open sometimes and reverse sometimes, so this key is not always valid.

Keying the guards is standard in the 5-2 (five down linemen, two linebackers) or 3-4 (three linemen, four linebackers) defense. The backer "mirrors" the action of the guard. If the guard attacks him, he attacks the guard and then pursues. If the guard drops back in pass protection, the backer drops into pass coverage. If the guard pulls behind his linemen, the backer moves behind his linemen. If the guard blocks the next man in or out, the backer steps into the same area in which the guard moved. Teams should practice these keys as often as possible.

Keying a running back is done similarly. If the back crosses the center, so does the linebacker. If the back attacks on his side of the center, the backer moves to that area. Generally the backer keys only the first step, but sometimes, in order to pick up counters, he keys for two or three steps. A "near back key" is used when the offensive team does not cross its back.

Keying a far back (cross key) is often used when the offensive team crosses its backs, such as in a cross buck or a belly series counter. The same principles apply as in keying a near back. If the far back comes at the backer, the backer holds and protects his responsibility. If the running back moves the other direction, the backer pursues.

In playing against an I-formation offense, the backer may be coached to key the fullback or the tailback. Usually he keys the back who is most likely to run a counter.

Reading through a lineman to a back is a more complicated read, but is often much more effective because it can pick up counter plays in which a lineman leads in counter plays. There is no reason to key linemen unless they lead in counters.

Reading through the near guard to the near back is the easier read. (However, it should not be used if the offense crosses its backs.) The backer should look through the guard to the near back. If the guard makes lateral movement, a pull, the backer honors that and starts laterally. If the guard moves forward, even at an angle, the backer disregards the guard and keys the back as explained above.

If a team crosses its backs and pulls one or both guards on counters, the backer should read through the near guard to the far back. He uses the same principles as above — lateral movement by the guard is primary; if no lateral movement, key the back.

If a team is a heavy keying defense, the players should use the "universal" read. It works against any offense, but it is the most difficult to master. The only exception to its success is when a team employs key breakers, such as false-pulling a guard or running the far side back away from the point of attack.

With practice, the universal read can be done effectively, but it is not a technique that can be mastered the week of a game. A heavy keying defense, if it is to be used, must be practiced all year.

Another type of key is called "reading a triangle." The triangle may be the guard, center, and near back or the guard, tackle, and near back. Some coaches prefer the guard, quarterback, and near back. In this read, the emphasis is on the blocking pattern of the linemen rather than the movement of the back.

Another possible assignment of the backer can be to "get" a back. In this assignment, he is responsible for stopping one back, whether it is a run or a pass. This assignment may be used in a man-to-man pass defense, or when one offensive back is a controlling type of player. When this is the case, one or both inside backers may be told that their only responsibility is to stop that player.

Playing the Block

The blocking scheme gives the inside backer an even better idea as to where the play is heading. The blockers may attack the inside backers in one of several ways. The backer must focus on the potential blockers rather than looking at the back. He can read the key and then look at the blockers, but if he looks for the ball carrier, he is likely to be blindsided by a blocker and knocked out of the play.

The drive block by the lineman directly ahead of the inside backer should be met with a shoulder charge and forearm rip by the inside shoulder and forearm. The inside leg should be forward. The target is the inside number of the lineman. From the snap of the ball, the backer should be checking the flow angle of the backs to tip off an inside or outside attack. Still, the backer must defeat the block before moving right or left.

If the backer is playing on the guard, as in a 5-2 or 3-4, he should squeeze the guard toward the center with his outside leverage (outside arm). He should not let the head of the guard get past the outside hip. If the ball goes outside, he must react and make the play from the inside out.

Overcoming Blocks

The cut block is a block aimed at the backer's knees or lower. If the lineman is not looking at the blocker, this can be an effective block. However if he sees the blocker coming low, he merely has to keep his feet back, put his hands on the back of the blocker, and push him down while giving ground slightly.

The reach or hook block has the lineman stepping outside to get an outside position on the backer. The backer must step wide with the outside leg in order to meet the blocker head up. He then plays the same technique as in the drive block.

The scoop or slip block has the lineman on the backer blocking the next defensive lineman toward the flow. The offensive man toward the flow is then free to slip his man and get a better angle on the backer. The key is that the offensive lineman on the backer moves directly down the line of scrimmage toward the backfield flow. The backer must step in the same direction and be ready to meet the next blocker. The player should meet the blocker with the near forearm and shoulder and then be ready for the cutback. If there is no cutback, he should take the best angle of pursuit — to either side of the blocker.

The cross block is expected when the lineman blocks down. The backer steps with his inside leg at a 45-degree angle toward the man who is attacking him. He makes the same type of hit, inside shoulder and forearm to inside number, squeezes the blocker into the hole with his outside leverage, then reacts to the ball carrier.

The down block should be met with the outside shoulder and forearm into the outside number of the down blocking lineman. Watch for a cutback by the ball carrier, then pursue.

The trap block is keyed when the lineman blocks down on the backer. The backer looks inside, expecting a pulling lineman to attempt to block him out. He meets it as with a cross block — inside shoulder and forearm to inside number of trapper. The blocker should squeeze the trapper into the hole. He must not let the trapper's head get past his outside hip. The blocker should make the play bounce outside.

Overcoming the cut block.

The fold block requires the backer to take a lateral step in order to meet the blocker head on. The backer should meet the blocker with the near shoulder and forearm and immediately pursue across the blocker's head.

The isolation block is keyed when the lineman blocks down or out and the near back or fullback is coming into the hole. He is played the same as a drive block — inside shoulder and forearm to inside number. He should then squeeze the back to the inside to make the play bounce out.

The pull and seal by the lineman is played by stepping laterally, hitting with the near shoulder and forearm, and checking for a blocking back or the ball carrier.

All of these blocks might not possible to simulate in practice, but players can certainly learn to recognize different blocks by focusing on the inside backer while watching a game on television or in person.

Blocking Progression

The inside backer must be aware of blocks coming from several areas. The concerns are, in this order:

1. Man on man outside

2. Man inside
3. Near back
4. Far guard
5. Near end, tackle, or flanker

The blocks he might expect are:

- From man on -- drive, scramble, cut, double team
- Near back -- lead, delayed double team
- Far guard -- trap
- Near end -- tackle, flanker in motion, seal

The pursuit path of the linebacker can be based on the instinct of the player or can be planned. If he has no other assignment than to make the tackle, the onside backer should pursue, keeping the runner on his outside shoulder. The offside backer should keep the runner about a yard ahead of him to prevent a cutback.

Players can be shown proper pursuit paths with plastic football players, or even stand-in devices such as salt shakers. A play can be set up and "run" by moving the pieces in motion. A player can then move the piece that represents himself in the proper pursuit angle. Budding linebackers also should watch the pursuit paths of players on television.

When the pursuit angle is planned as part of the defensive assignment, it can be into the line or behind the line. When the backer's responsibility calls for him to move into a hole in the line, it is called a "scrape" or "scrape off." When his responsibility calls for him to remain on his side of the line of scrimmage until he has a clear shot at the ball carrier, it is called a "shuffle."

Many defenses are designed to have the onside backer scrape into a hole created by the placement or the charge of the defensive linemen. This is really a controlled stunt. The backer doesn't know where he will penetrate until he has read his key. As he moves into the hole, he must spot the ball carrier, stay slightly behind him to eliminate a cutback, then attack the ball.

The shuffling linebacker moves behind the line of scrimmage, staying about a yard behind the ball carrier. When he sees an opening, he can move across the line and make or assist on the tackle. In shuffling, it is important to keep the shoulders square to the line of scrimmage and to move without crossing the legs for as long a distance as possible.

Playing off blockers is often essential to get to the ball, but the backer should remember that his job is to make the tackle — not to play off blockers. Fighting the pressure is easier for linebackers because they are farther from their attackers and have more room to maneuver. Most defensive assignments expect the linebackers to have an outside responsibility. Because of this, they generally use one of two techniques.

The backer may play the blocker with a forearm flipper using the inside forearm and keeping the outside arm free to control the outside of the blocker. This is more often used if the blocker is upright.

Against lower blockers or those coming at an angle, the backer may use the hands to ward off the blocker, always making certain to control the outside of the blocker. The hands should control the shoulder pads as the backer concentrates on the blocker while "seeing" the ball carrier.

As with defensive linemen, the backer should fight through the blocker's head. It is permissible for a backer to give a little ground as he plays through the head and continues his lateral movement.

When the blocker is coming from directly in front of the backer and the ball carrier is directly behind the blocker, the backer must defeat the blocker while not taking a side. The forearm rip is generally the most effective technique to use. He should straighten up the blocker, push him away with the free (outside) hand, and make the tackle. He should never spin in this situation.

XV. Linebacker Play Against the Pass

Pass defense is a prime responsibility of the linebackers. They usually are called to drop into a specific zone, but they are also called upon to play man-to-man defense.

Zone Defense

Pass drops begin when the backer picks up his pass key. For the inside backer, it may be the linemen setting in cup protection; for an outside backer, it may be his tight end releasing. Most coaches teach their players to turn to the outside and run back to the assigned zone while watching the eyes of the quarterback. Coaches also generally ask the backer to peek at the near receivers to get a tip on the pattern that will be run. If he sees a wideout (flanker) starting to curl in, the backer may adjust to a wider and deeper spot than he had anticipated. If he sees the wideout running a quick slant, he may adjust to a shorter and wider position.

The most important concern should be the eyes of the quarterback. For this reason, some coaches don't want their players to peek at the potential receivers. They merely get their keys from the eyes of the passer. Few passers at the high school, or even the college, level do a good job of "looking off" the backers. This is especially true if there is an effective pass rush.

When reading the eyes, the backer starts to make his drop, but adjusts the drop depending on where the passer looks. By watching the eyes effectively, four short defenders at a 10-yard depth should be able to cover the entire width of the field. The problem, of course, is to be able to get to the proper depth.

Traditionally, the proper depth has been 10 yards. As 15- to 18-yard patterns have become more common, the drops have often been adjusted to compensate for these patterns. Some coaches have their backers drop immediately to the 10-yard depth and then count "1001, 1002" and start drifting farther back. The thinking is that if the pattern is a 10-yard "hook" or "in" pattern, it would have been thrown by the time the backer gets to the 10-yard depth. The backer can drift deeper to reduce the seam between himself and the defensive backs and help on the deeper curl patterns or the deep across patterns.

Reading the eyes of the quarterback can give the backer a big jump on the direction of the pass. As with so many other factors in football, the coach must choose between having him peek at the receivers or reacting only to the eyes of the quarterback. It is obvious that if he is peeking at receivers, he has lost eye contact with the passer and may miss the early jump that he could have had if he had not been watching the receivers. Some coaches maintain that the backers cannot really see the eyes, so they must look at the face guard or jaw of the passer.

Backers can get the jump on the ball if they move immediately as the passer looks at his target. Some coaches teach to start slowly and then run fast as the passer takes his long step. Most coaches teach the backers to run fast at the target when they see the passer's look. They should keep their eyes on the quarterback while running. Other coaches teach to look at the target and run as fast as possible toward the target as soon as the key is recognized. This assures that the backer can cover the greatest distance towards the target.

Coaches must determine whether they want the backers to jump on the passer's eye key or to protect against a possible throwback. The choice is between reckless pursuit and caution.

Players can practice reading the eyes by having one player play the quarterback and another play an inside linebacker. As the quarterback drops to pass, the linebacker drops to his zone. The quarterback looks right or left, and the backer should turn his body that way and then move in the direction the quarterback is looking. The quarterback should use the proper stepping technique. He can then throw the ball about five yards outside of where the linebacker is moving.

As the linebackers get better at reading the quarterback's eyes, the quarterback can look one way, then the other and throw in the second direction. The linebacker can even be made to adjust three times to the quarterback's looks, if it is a long pass. The quarterback can look right, left, then right again before throwing to the deep curl area.

Being conscious of the receivers is the other option for the backer. If he can see the potential receiver, he should work to get about three yards in front of and no more than three yards inside of the receiver. If no receiver is near him, he can begin backpedaling and look for nearby receivers.

The backers should tell each other where the receivers are and who may be entering their zone. "Curl behind" or "deep cross" are examples of alerting an adjacent linebacker.

Man-to-Man Pass Defense

The backer must know whether he has deep help from the safeties or whether he must cover his man all over the field. If his assignment is to take away the underneath patterns (up to 18 yards), he can play more recklessly. In this assignment, he can play under the man and knock down or intercept any short passes. If he has no secondary defenders behind him, he must play more cautiously.

With deep help, he can align himself inside and at a depth of six inches to four yards while playing a receiver wider than a tight end. He should not let the receiver inside of him. A tight end, wingback, or inside slot back should be played close and slightly inside.

The backer should concentrate on the receiver, chucking him, and keeping him outside. If he is playing tight to the line of scrimmage, as in a bump and run, he must slow the receiver's pattern and knock him out of the pattern by making him run laterally rather than up the field. He must then stay on the inside hip of the receiver.

If the defender is off the ball, he maintains his inside position. If the receiver tries to cross inside, the defender hits him. He should try to remain two to three yards deeper than the receiver and a yard to his inside. He should duplicate the receiver's cuts while maintaining the "air cushion" between himself and the receiver. If the receiver gets behind him he plays the same technique as the bump and run player and gets on the receiver's inside hip.

The defender must be as close to the receiver as possible, continually looking at the receiver. He looks for the ball on one or all of the following keys: when the receiver looks for the ball, when the receiver's eyes are obviously concentrating on the ball (they usually widen), or when the receiver's hands move up to get into position to catch the ball.

Defenders can practice against receivers running simulated routes. They should hit the receiver as soon as he leaves the line of scrimmage, and then try to duplicate the receiver's patterns. When the receiver gets behind the defender, the defender should try to stay in the receiver's hip pocket -- between the receiver and the passer. When the receiver raises his hands or widens his eyes, the defender should turn and look for the ball.

If the backer's assignment is a running back, the backer checks for an immediate release by the back. If the back sets to block, the backer goes to him and plays him with his hands, which does two things: the back is occupied and cannot block a defensive lineman, and the backer is close to the back and behind the blockers in case the back releases for a screen pass.

XVI. Outside Linebackers Against the Run

The stance for an outside backer playing on a tight end or an inside slot back usually is lower than that of an inside backer so that the outside backer can meet the potential block of the nearest opponent.

Alignment should be closer to the line of scrimmage, usually as close as possible if a blocker is an immediate threat, such as a tight end or slotback. If the outside blocker is playing wider, such as in a walkaway position (half way out toward a wide receiver), he may drop off a few yards.

Contact is generally done with a hand shiver. The hands are driven under the shoulder pads of the offensive player, and the player is lifted and controlled as the backer reads the keys. It is important to not allow the offensive end or slot back to release inside. Releasing enables the offensive player to help the tackle on a double team block or seal off an inside linebacker. It also frees him to catch a quick pass from the quarterback.

Keys for outside backers usually start with the nearest two lineman and then the near back. If the backer is playing on a tight end, he reads the end and tackle and then the near back. If the end releases, it is likely to be a pass or a run away from the backer's side. The end is the major key.

Before the snap, the backer should recognize which plays can be run at him from the backfield set. A wide halfback gives the offense the possibility of a quick pitch. With this possibility, the backer must be alert to the pull of the tackle leading the pitch. With backs in a veer set (behind or slightly wider than the guards), the linebacker should be alert to the veer attacking his area and then play his assignment — either the dive back, the quarterback option, or the pitch. Against an I-formation, the backer needs to be aware of an off-tackle play, or perhaps a quarterback option play. If a halfback is behind the tackle on his side, he may expect to help out on a dive play, but an option is also a possibility. If a halfback is not nearby, but is on the other side, the backer should be alert for the sweep or cross buck.

In looking at his triangle, the outside linebacker must be alert for the end and tackle blocking down. This probably indicates a trap, so he must prepare to meet it. If it is a veer set or a wishbone, he must be ready to play the option if the linemen block down.

Most coaches assign the linebacker on the tight end to keep the end off of the middle backer in a seal block and to slow the end on pass plays.

The outside backer must be alert to several types of blocks and plays aimed at the off-tackle area or wider. He must be alert to the drive block, the kick out block, and the reach block from linemen. He must be aware of a block from a back that can be designed to take him in (log) or out. He also must be alert to the sweep, quick pitch, and the option. Generally the outside backer reacts to the step of the tight end on him. If he is a weak side backer with no one on him, he will have more time to read his keys and to react.

Playing the drive block is done by stepping with the inside foot, striking under the shoulders with the hands or forearm, then bringing the hips closer to the blocker so that the blocker can be lifted. If using the hands, the outside linebacker should lock out the arms, then react to the pressure or the keys. He should control the line of scrimmage and not be driven back. The blocker should be controlled with the outside hand and squeeze him inside, thus reducing the off-tackle hole. By keeping outside leverage, he can pursue the wide runs from the inside out.

Linebackers can be taught to react to the drive block — the most common block they will encounter — by working with another player in an offensive stance. The linebacker assumes the two-point linebacker's stance in front of the other player. He should be low enough to be able to get his hands on the other player's chest (under where the shoulder pads would be). The other player (the blocker) takes a step forward in slow motion. The linebacker steps to meet him. The linebacker's hips should be low so that he can lift the blocker with his legs. He should hit the blocker on the low part of the chest. The fingers should be spread, the wrists close together, and the elbows pointed down. He should lift with his legs and his arms.

Next, linebackers should learn to fight the pressure of the block. The rule for defensive players is to never go behind the back of a blocker, always go across the face to get to the ball. To work on this reaction, one player can play the blocker and put his head to one side of the linebacker's shoulder. The linebacker should put his hands on the blocker's chest, as if he is hitting the blocker, and then move across his face. The linebacker must not cross his legs. He must stay in a good low "football" position, taking short and quick steps as he moves across the blocker's face.

Playing the reach block is done by stepping laterally as the tight end steps laterally to get an outside position. The backer hits with his hands into the shoulder pads of the end and keeps the end's shoulder pads from turning him inside. An effective outside backer turns the blocker's outside shoulder away from the line, making it impossible to be hooked in. The end must not be allowed to get an angled position on the backer and wall him off from an outside play.

This reaction can be learned by having one player line up as the tight end. The backer lines up directly in front of the tight end or slightly to the outside. The tight end takes a lateral step with the outside leg to get outside of the backer. The backer hits the tight end with his hands while moving his feet quickly to stay outside of the other player. He should work to get the tight end's outside shoulder pushed away from the line of scrimmage so that the tight end can't block the backer in. The backer keeps his feet moving quickly while keeping an outside position on the tight end.

Playing the pulling lineman is done by stepping into the end, who is blocking down, and controlling him with a hand shiver, knocking him off of the lineman to his inside, probably the defensive end. The backer should check the flow of the backs and the depth of the pulling lineman to determine if they are attempting to run off tackle (to his inside) or wide. Guards pulling deeper or a back taking a looping path toward him (to log him in) indicate a wide play.

If the play is designed to run inside, the backer should control the end with the inside forearm and outside hand or both hands. He should close the hole down from the outside. If the play is going wide, he must avoid being logged in by a back or pulling lineman by using his hands and keeping his feet free as he strings out the play.

Backers can practice against the trap block by having another player start in either guard's position. The guard pulls parallel with the line of scrimmage. (He should sometimes move toward the line of scrimmage, which is what good guards are taught to do.) The backer pretends he is playing against an end who is blocking down toward the tackle. He moves toward the tackle, and then, as he sees the guard, he plays the guard with both hands or with his inside forearm flipper while using his outside hand to help to control the guard — keeping the hole to the guard's inside as small as possible.

Playing the cross block of the end and tackle is done by controlling the end, keeping him off the inside defender, then closing the hole and meeting the tackle with the hands or an inside forearm. This block is recognized by seeing the tackle come directly at him from over the hip of the downblocking end.

Blocking Progression

A drill can be set up with a few players, or the players can do it at home on a table, using household objects for players. It is important that the outside backer get used to expecting blocks from every direction and be ready to play each blocker correctly.

Which blocks should the outside backer expect from each potential blocker? The most likely types are listed below. In drills, the blockers should alternate these techniques so that the backers can become proficient at recognizing and playing all of the potential blocks. These drills should be done in slow motion to prevent injury.

Blocks to expect:

- From man on—drive, cut, hook (reach)
- From man outside—double team, angle
- From man inside—angle
- From near guard—trap
- From near back—lead, log, delayed double team
- From far guard—trap, log

Playing the release of the tight end requires that the backer hit him to knock him off his path. If he releases inside, the backer should step down with him. The height of the end's head may tip off the type of play, run or pass. If the end's head is low, he is probably blocking for a run. If his head is high, he is probably releasing for a pass.

The outside release may signal a pass, an option play, or a run to the other side. The backer hits the end and then looks to the inside to find the ball.

To work on playing the release, a player acting as the end can step directly into the backer as if he is blocking. The end sometimes releases inside, sometimes outside. The end should start in slow motion so that the backer can perfect the technique.

Playing the option depends on the theory of the defense being used. In some defenses, the backer attacks the quarterback making him pitch quickly. In other defenses, he may be required to "slow play" the quarterback. In slow playing him, the backer remains on the line of scrimmage in a position where the quarterback has trouble cutting back on him. The backer strings the play out as the defensive pursuit forms and the ball approaches the 12th man, the sideline.

General responsibilities of backers' stunts (or blitzes) give linebackers the opportunities to make big plays. In a stunt, the linebacker attacks the assigned area on the snap of the ball, either continuing through the hole or making a read as he attacks and adjusting his charge based on the read. For example, if the stunt is designed to work against a drop back pass but the offense runs a quick pitch, the linebacker adjusts and gets into a proper pursuit path rather than continuing toward the quarterback.

The stunting backer should not tip off the offense that he is blitzing. He must start on the snap of the ball and charge toward his hole responsibility. As he approaches the hole, he should adjust to the movement of the linemen or the backfield action. If the guards pull, he should follow them. If they set in pass protection, he should attack and use the techniques of pass rush described previously. He should know whether he has an inside rushing lane or outside containment on the pass.

XVII. Defensive Secondary Play

The players in the defensive secondary, the cornerbacks and safeties, must be intelligent and skilled. They are the last line of defense to prevent touchdowns. Their techniques depend on the defensive theory of the coach whether they play man-to-man or zone, loose or tight, deep or shallow. In any case, they must keep mistakes to a minimum.

The secondary rules should be very simple to reduce errors. Some coaches teach only one defense, with the defensive backs never varying in assignment. This reduces errors, but it also reduces the ability to change the coverage and keep the offense off-balance. At the lower levels of football, simple rules are best.

Coaches should commit to a defensive style before the season starts, so that the players can become more proficient at it. There are a few skills all defensive players use, however, and they should devote a great deal of time to them.

The stance should be a comfortable two-point stance. A "bump and run" cornerback would have both feet parallel or near parallel. If taking away one side of a receiver by moving slightly inside or outside, the bump and run player might play the foot nearest to the receiver slightly closer to the line of scrimmage. Backs playing deeper might play in a similar stance but with the inside foot back.

The bump and run player should have his hands up ready to hit the receiver. Backs playing deeper can keep their arms more relaxed. The closer the defensive back is to the receiver, the more important the stance.

The alignment of the backs depends on their responsibility. Some coaches prefer that they line up the same on every play to reduce the pre-snap read of the quarterback and receivers. Other coaches want the back to line up so that their assignments will be easier to carry out.

In a normal zone or man-to-man defense, the free safety may be 10 to 15 yards deep. The strong safety may be two to 10 yards deep and one to two yards outside of the tight end. The corners may be as deep as 10 yards, but usually at a five- to eight-yard depth. The corners may play slightly outside or inside the receiver, depending on the width of the receiver and the responsibility of the defender.

The bump and run player should be very close to the line of scrimmage, one foot to two yards.

Responsibilities of the defensive secondary depend on whether they are playing a zone defense, a man-to-man defense, or a combination of the two. In the zone defense, the defensive back should get to his area while watching the passer. The depth that he plays is determined by the zone he is assigned to cover.

In the man-to-man defense, the defensive back's major concern is to cover a particular man. The depth that he plays depends on whether he is playing bump and run or playing "off him," giving the receiver a cushion of air and not enabling him to complete the deep pass. If giving him a cushion, he generally plays five to seven yards deep.

Jamming the potential receiver is a technique used in man-to-man bump and run defense and in some zone defenses, such as when the corner has a shallow zone pass responsibility. The technique is similar to the hand shiver used by defensive linemen, but is generally made from the inside out or the outside in. The hit should be made with the palms open and the thumbs up. The blow should be struck low in the numbers up and through the receiver. Straightening him up throws him off his path and hinders the timing of the pass. The jam also can be done with the defender hitting the center of the receiver's chest with the hand nearest to the receiver.

The defensive back should be able to maintain his balance, so he should not overextend into the hit. However, when he knows that he has effective help in the deep zone, he can unload on the potential receiver as long as he can keep his balance.

The defender should try to run the receiver out of his route and slow the timing of the pattern. Because the receiver will be trying to get into his planned route, the longer the receiver is delayed, the more the overall pattern is disrupted and the greater the chance for a sack of the quarterback. If the defensive back can force the receiver to run along the line of scrimmage, the receiver has been effectively delayed.

Most bumps will be made with one hand only. This stops the defender from over-extending into the hit. The hand that hits will be the hand farthest from the direction that the receiver is moving. This enables the defender to open up in the same direction that the receiver is moving.

Zone responsibilities require that either two or three defensive backs cover deep. If three backs are used, they generally play the three deep zones if it is a drop back pass. They may rotate into a two deep set on a long sprint out or roll out pass if the defensive halfback on the side of the flow is given the assignment of the flat zone. With two safeties and two corners, many combinations are possible to cover two or three deep zones.

If flow goes away from the defensive halfback (three deep) or the corner (four deep) he should remain cautious of the bootleg, reverse, reverse pass, counter action, or play action pass. His rotation should not continue until he is certain that there is no possibility of a play coming back to his area.

Defensive backs should concentrate only on the play of the back who plays their position when they watch games. They can write down when the back reacts too quickly to pursuit on plays away or when he comes up too fast on a run fake to aid in their study.

Man to man responsibilities can be either bump and run, a press technique, or playing off the receiver with a cushion of air.

In a bump and run technique, the defensive back will take away the underneath patterns by playing between the passer and the receiver. This is called "trailing." The long pass is taken away because of the speed of the defender. If the team is playing bump and run with the deep zones covered, the speed of the corner is not as critical.

Bump and run technique.

Playing the option depends on the theory of the defense being used. In some defenses, the backer attacks the quarterback making him pitch quickly. In other defenses, he may be required to "slow play" the quarterback. In slow playing him, the backer remains on the line of scrimmage in a position where the quarterback has trouble cutting back on him. The backer strings the play out as the defensive pursuit forms and the ball approaches the 12th man, the sideline.

General responsibilities of backers' stunts (or blitzes) give linebackers the opportunities to make big plays. In a stunt, the linebacker attacks the assigned area on the snap of the ball, either continuing through the hole or making a read as he attacks and adjusting his charge based on the read. For example, if the stunt is designed to work against a drop back pass but the offense runs a quick pitch, the linebacker adjusts and gets into a proper pursuit path rather than continuing toward the quarterback.

The stunting backer should not tip off the offense that he is blitzing. He must start on the snap of the ball and charge toward his hole responsibility. As he approaches the hole, he should adjust to the movement of the linemen or the backfield action. If the guards pull, he should follow them. If they set in pass protection, he should attack and use the techniques of pass rush described in Chapter 14. He should know whether he has an inside rushing lane or outside containment on the pass.

Playing the option depends on the theory of the defense being used. In some defenses, the backer attacks the quarterback making him pitch quickly. In other defenses, he may be required to "slow play" the quarterback. In slow playing him, the backer remains on the line of scrimmage in a position where the quarterback has trouble cutting back on him. The backer strings the play out as the defensive pursuit forms and the ball approaches the 12th man, the sideline.

General responsibilities of backers' stunts (or blitzes) give linebackers the opportunities to make big plays. In a stunt, the linebacker attacks the assigned area on the snap of the ball, either continuing through the hole or making a read as he attacks and adjusting his charge based on the read. For example, if the stunt is designed to work against a drop back pass but the offense runs a quick pitch, the linebacker adjusts and gets into a proper pursuit path rather than continuing toward the quarterback.

The stunting backer should not tip off the offense that he is blitzing. He must start on the snap of the ball and charge toward his hole responsibility. As he approaches the hole, he should adjust to the movement of the linemen or the backfield action. If the guards pull, he should follow them. If they set in pass protection, he should attack and use the techniques of pass rush described previosly. He should know whether he has an inside rushing lane or outside containment on the pass.

In the "press" technique, the defender plays up to a yard-and-a-half off the receiver. He backpedals with the receiver, then as the receiver makes his cut, the defender hits him with his "far" arm, the arm away from the direction of the cut. This hit should slow the receiver a bit and also help to turn the defender so that he can run with the receiver.

When using the press technique, many coaches teach that the primary responsibility is inside. If a receiver has cut inside and then outside, the defender is told to honor the inside fake (on a double cut pattern) and then to turn away from the receiver to get depth as he relocates the receiver on his outside. Double cut patterns such as a post-square out (a "dig" pattern) or a post-curl out will leave the receiver open. However, the more dangerous post-corner would have a good chance of being well covered.

If a team's defensive theory requires the defensive back to play off the line, he will not have as much responsibility for the very short passes, but will be asked to take away the intermediate routes and still play the deep routes. However, he may also have a safety behind him for the deep routes so he can play the intermediate routes more aggressively. When playing "off the line," coaches require the defender to "shade" one side or the other playing about a yard inside or outside of the receiver and taking away one possible cut. Most often they take away the outside cut, inviting the receiver to cut into the middle of the field where the linebackers may provide help.

The press technique.

Zone techniques start with using whatever depth is necessary to get to the proper zone. This must be done prior to the snap of the ball. If a safety in a three-deep alignment is required to

The three steps and turn drill.

cover the deep outside zone in a rotation (against a sprint out or roll out) he may start 12 to 15 yards deep. On the other hand, a corner who is required to cover the deep zone directly behind him may be able to line up six to eight yards deep and still have plenty of time to get to his zone.

The first steps of the defensive back in most defenses are backward. Some teams have the defender turn and shuffle or start to run into his zone, because it is faster, but today it is more common to backpedal toward the zone. In either case, he will be reading his keys for directions to run or pass as he takes his first steps. If he "reads" his key and it predicts a running play, he can forget his zone and play his run responsibility. If he is in doubt, he plays the pass.

If running backward into the zone, the defender must have the agility to turn right or left whenever the quarterback looks in that direction.

The three steps and turn drill is essential to zone defense, and is also an excellent agility drill. The player starts his step with his left leg, moving at a 45-degree angle to his left rear. His next step is a crossover step with his right leg. The next step is with the left leg. As the left toe hits the ground, he makes a three-quarters turn to the right on the ball of his foot and then steps backward to his right with his right leg, then a left leg crossover, then a right step, then another 270 degree pivot. He will face the quarterback on each move. As players become more comfortable with the movement, they can increase speed. He also increases his angle of running so that eventually he can do this drill going straight back.

The three step and turn drill can be taught by having players walk through it first. They should pause after each step at first to check their form. On all three steps, the feet should be pointing directly the way the player is running. On the third step, the 270- degree pivot should be made back toward the line of scrimmage until the foot is pointing directly in the direction it will run.

Backpedaling is the more common technique used today. The backpedal is preferred because it enables the defender to keep his original alignment and leverage on the receiver. It keeps the defender's shoulders parallel to the line of scrimmage and enables him to move forward, right, or left quickly, and it is more effective than the shuffle if playing a loose man-to-man coverage.

The technique of the backpedal requires that the defender keep his torso forward with his chin over his toes and his shoulders over his knees. The head should be down, and the elbows bent at 90 degrees. The steps are made quickly while driving the arms hard. By keeping the head and torso forward, he should remain balanced and be able to stop and break forward for any short pass. The feet should be no wider than the hips. The player should concentrate on "stepping back" rather than "pushing off" because emphasizing pushing back may force him to lean back on his heels and make him stand up straighter, both of which will slow him down.

A defensive back should backpedal at 3/4 speed. If he were at full speed, he would not be able to change directions as fast if he had to come up for a run or to break forward for a short pass. The steps should be small to medium in length. The feet should stay close to the ground. The knees should be bent to allow the feet to reach back. The arms should pump forward and back, not across the body.

As the player backpedals, he should remain in the proper leverage position, usually outside, in order to take away one of the receiver's options in cutting. After the receiver cuts, the defender should whip his near arm toward the direction he will be running. This helps him to change directions more quickly.

Defensive backs should practice backpedaling straight back, in a weave pattern and at 30- and 45-degree angles to their initial straight drop. They must continually work on keeping the cushion (at least three yards) and the shade (at least one yard) on the receiver. To work on the backpedal, players should bend their knees slightly, bend forward at the waist, have their head over their toes, then step backward. They should do this one step at a time in slow motion, making certain their form is perfect: the feet are as wide as the shoulders, elbows in a 90-degree flex, head over the toes, eyes up. The emphasis should be on stepping backward, not pushing off.

First, practice moving straight back. This movement should be perfect before the back moves faster. After the back is up to speed, he can start to weave backwards, moving in an "S" line.

The speed and depth of the drop depends on the team's defensive theory. Some coaches prefer that the defensive back be much deeper than the receivers. If using this theory, the back is much more likely to be able to intercept the long ball or to react more effectively laterally to any long ball.

The deeper the defender is before the release of the pass, the more he can get under control as the passer sets and the greater lateral distance he can cover after the ball is released. Of course if he is very deep, the seam between him and the more shallow pass coverage will be greater. The advantage to playing closer to the receiver is that the defender is closer to the target area if the pass is thrown into the intermediate zone of 15 to 22 yards.

Whichever theory is utilized, the defender must watch the quarterback. While many coaches have the defender peek at the receivers in his area, doing so may take away the defender's ability to react quickly to the eyes or arm of the passer. It generally takes more than a second to change focus from peeking at a receiver to establishing contact with the passer's eyes.

Some coaches have their defensive backs turn their bodies and even move a bit in the direction that the passer is looking. However, the main key to release the defender to go to the ball is the "long arm action" of the passer. Most passers fake a pass with a short arm action and a short step. When making a long pass their arms come back farther and they take a longer step. By watching the "long arm" action of the passer, the defender can start to go in the direction of the pass before it is thrown.

After the ball is in the air, the defender should move to the area in which he can intercept it at the highest point. Since he will have a greater depth than the offensive receiver (at least five yards), he should have more room to maneuver for the ball than the receiver who is running at top speed to the point of reception.

Several drills can help defensive backs who play in a zone defensive system. Regardless of the team's defensive theory, backs probably should be encouraged to play a little deeper. Players generally want to play closer to the receivers than they are taught to do.

The line drill is used to teach a defensive back to cover farther to his side. He should start about 10 yards away from the quarterback. If there is a line, such as a sideline or a yard stripe, use it.

As the quarterback starts to drop back to pass, the defensive back should backpedal quickly along the line. As the quarterback looks in one direction, the defensive back should turn his body that way. (Refer to the three steps and turn drill.) The quarterback should throw the ball away from the defensive back and let him go for it. At first the quarterback should throw the ball five yards from the back's backpedal path. Then he should throw seven yards away from him, then 10, 12, and 15. Eventually, when the players are in high school, backs should be able to catch balls thrown 20 yards away from them.

The defensive back should be sure to catch the ball at the highest point. If he catches it low, the imaginary receiver would have caught it at a higher point.

If three kids are available, one receiver can be placed on each side of the defensive back. They should start five yards outside of him. As he gets better, the receivers can move seven to 10 yards outside of him, or more. The receivers start downfield while the defender retreats. The quarterback then throws to either receiver. This drill shows the defensive back that he can cover a wide lateral area if he has sufficient depth and reacts on the long arm action of the passer. The drill can also be done across the width of the field, with the receivers running on yardlines 10, 15, and then 20 yards apart and the defender on the yardline between them.

Running backward and reacting to the ball. This drill can be done backpedaling or running. The player gets to his zone and continues backward. As the passer looks, the defender turns his body in the direction that the passer is looking. When the passer makes the "long arm" action of the pass, the defender breaks for the ball in the direction that the passer is stepping.

The tip drill is used to help a player stay alert to the ball. Someone throws the ball, then another player tips it. The ball should be tipped in a variety of ways. The defensive back can be running backward or crossways behind the tipper in this drill.

Playing through the receiver to get to the ball is essential. After the ball is in the air it belongs to either team. Neither team can interfere with the other. Interference occurs only when one player plays the man rather than the ball.

This can be practiced at a walk-through pace. The defensive back can attack the receiver from behind. If someone is available to toss the ball, the defensive back can get used to going for it through the receiver's body.

Catching the ball should be done by squaring the shoulders to the ball, reaching or jumping high (catching the ball at its highest point), looking the ball into the hands, and catching the near end of the ball. If the defender concentrates on catching the end of the ball it won't go through his hands. If it were to bounce out of his hands and forward, he still would have an opportunity to catch it after he had blocked it. Obviously if it goes through his hands, he has no second chance at making the interception.

After making the interception and tucking the ball under his arm, the defender yells a code word, such as "oskie" or "fire," to alert his teammates that he has intercepted and that they should block for him.

Running into the ball gives the defender practice on catching the ball when moving into it. The speed of the pass can be increased as players become more adept at catching. Players can improve their ability to catch by reaching for the ball and giving with it to cushion it.

Verbal communication on the pass is essential. The sequence is:

- "Pass" when it is recognized that a pass is being thrown.
- "Ball" when the ball is in the air.

Catching the ball.

- "Got it" when the defender knows he can intercept it. This alerts the nearby teammates to get ready to block for him or to be ready for a tipped ball. Sometimes two defenders are in position to intercept but knock each other off the interception because of lack of communication.
- "Oskie" or "fire" after the interception has been made and the ball tucked away. This alerts the teammates to block. Players should yell the appropriate key word at the right time. They can practice this at home while watching television or during doing the drills.

In addition to the above verbal commands, the backs should call out the patterns in front of them as they unfold. By calling "slant," "hook," "out," "in," "comeback," or "curl" the backers have a better chance of adjusting their drops and making the interception or deflecting the ball.

Watching the receiver's head and hands tells the defender when to look for the ball. Some coaches have the defender concentrate on the turn of the head and the focusing of the receiver's eyes. The eyes may open wider as the ball approaches. Other coaches have the defender watch the hands and arms. As the arms come up in preparation for the catch, the defender turns and looks for the ball. The defender's teammates should help by calling "ball" as the ball is released.

After the ball is in the air, the defender plays the ball. His inside position gives him an effective advantage in intercepting or batting down the ball, if he has remained close to the receiver. If the defender does not turn to play the ball and the ball hits him, he may be called for pass interference because he was playing the man rather than the ball. This is particularly true if the defender sees the arms raise and he raises his arms to block the receiver's vision without looking for the ball.

In practice, only one player should play a receiver. The defender should hit the receiver in the chest with one or both arms. If the receiver is directly in front of the defender, he can hit the receiver with both arms. If the receiver has been able to start diagonally up the field, the defender should hit the receiver with the arm farthest from the direction the receiver is cutting. Hitting with the farthest arm delays the receiver slightly, and it helps the defender make his turn as he covers the receiver.

The man-for-man defender must be particularly conscious of the types of patterns that should work most effectively against him the out and up, the hook and go, the post-corner, and the lean-in (on the defender) and break-out. The double fake is better countered by watching the eyes. The adept receiver may raise his hands on a fake (the hook, the out, or the post move of the double cut pattern), but his eyes will not bulge in anticipation of the catch.

Each of the above cuts can be run against defensive players in practice. Like anything else, the more they practice their techniques, the better they will become.

Stripping the ball from the receiver should be attempted as the ball is caught or after it has hit his hands. When the receiver has his back to the defender, such as in a hook pattern, the defender can bump him hard with his chest while bringing his hands under the elbows of the receiver and ripping the arms outward and upward. This is called "playing through the receiver." The defender's contact should occur just as the ball contacts the receiver, not before.

Another type of strip on a hook or comeback type of pattern comes from top to bottom, with the defender bringing his arms around the receiver and downward, attempting to make contact with the ball and forcing it downward.

When stripping from the side, the defender should grab at the receiver's far arm with his own far arm. So when going to the right, he should grab the receiver's right arm with his left arm. The reason to go for the far arm is that it is the hand on the far arm that is primarily responsible for stopping the ball on the catch.

If the far arm of the receiver cannot be reached, the defender can reach with his far arm for the near arm of the receiver while wrapping up the receiver with the far arm and making the tackle. If he is moving to his right and the receiver is moving and ahead of him, he can reach for the receiver's left arm with his left arm while wrapping up the receiver with his right arm. This is more effective if the ball is thrown ahead of the receiver and he is reaching for it. The near arm of the defender (the right arm in this example) hooks over the receiver's far shoulder.

These techniques often are ignored during team practices. They can be practiced individually with family members or friends at home.

Goal Line Play

The closer the offensive team moves to the goal line, the closer the defenders must play the receivers. Most teams play a tight man- to-man, even a bump and run, type of defense in this area. The defensive secondary, therefore, must be aware of pick plays with a flanker and tight end or two tight ends crossing.

When watching a game on television or in person, players should watch what defenses do when they are on the goal line, checking for what types of runs and passes they use. Players should be mentally ready to play on the goal line.

Stripping the ball.

Players should be alert for the pass at all times. Teams are likely to pass under the following circumstances:

- after a timeout
- after penalties on the defensive team
- at the end of the half or game, if behind
- after a substitution
- after a sudden change of possession (fumble, interception, long kick return)
- on first and ten, especially in four-down territory
- on second and short
- on third and long
- after an injury to a defensive back or linebacker

Run Responsibilities

Run responsibilities begin when the defender recognizes that the play is not a pass or when he recognizes that the pass is thrown out of his area.

When playing a zone defense, the defensive back should think pass as the ball is snapped. When it is apparent that a running play has been called, the defender adjusts his backward movement and begins moving forward or laterally into the proper rotation or pursuit path. The man-to-man defender must listen for verbal instructions from teammates to alert him whether a pass or run has been called. If the ball is being run, the defensive back must leave his coverage assignment and pursue the ball carrier.

Whether a defensive back is playing man-to-man or zone, if the pass is thrown into another area, the defender must sprint to the area in the hope of:

- making the tackle if the pass is complete
- catching the tipped ball if it is short and tipped by a linebacker, or long and tipped by the receiver or the covering back
- stripping the ball if it is caught by the receiver
- recovering a fumble if one occurs
- blocking for a teammate if he has intercepted the ball; the receiver should be the first target for a block

Supporting the run responsibilities depend on the defensive theory of the coach. The cornerback might have the wide responsibility on a sweep or option, but that responsibility can be given to a safety. The safety might be able to read the run more quickly because he is more likely to be playing a zone or, if in a man-to-man defense, watching the tight end on his side.

The backs away from the point of attack should take the path necessary to make certain that they can make the tackle if necessary. This requires a deeper angle for the backs farthest from the point of attack.

Defensive backs must never be knocked down. They have plenty of room in which to maneuver and should use their hands to play off the block.

Playing the blocker is another skill defensive backs must master. Often the defensive back has room to maneuver around the blocker who is moving fast. A simple fake one way and a move the other may be sufficient to get the blocker out of the way and be ready to make the tackle. This can be used if the ball carrier is some distance from the blocker.

If the blocking is well-timed and the ball carrier is close to the blocker, the defensive back must meet and defeat the blocker. When this is necessary, the defender must drop his weight over the leg with which he makes his lift, usually the inside leg. He anchors his back leg to absorb the hit of the blocker, gets his pads under the blocker's and rips with the arm over the forward leg. The other arm, usually the outside arm, punches up through the blocker's shoulder. The elbow must stay close to the body and under the shoulder. The palm and fingers should be up.

For defensive backs to practice defeating a block, a player is needed to play the blocker position. The blocker should hold a stiff pillow or some other sort of pad and walk slowly toward the defensive back. The back is instructed to protect either his right or his left side. If he is protecting the area of the field to his right, he should have his left foot forward and under him. His right leg is back to brace him against the power of the block. As he makes contact, he rips up and through the blocker with the left arm (a forearm rip) and the right hand. He also can play the blocker with both of his hands driving up and through the blocker's shoulder pads.

Tackling must be "sure" in the secondary. For this reason, the defensive backs can tackle high. They should be adept at working the high form tackle. They must be able to slow the ball carrier to enable the pursuit to catch up.

When tackling, the defensive back is not concerned with knocking the ball carrier backward, but with "wrapping him up" with his arms or forcing him out of bounds. The defensive back should never allow the ball carrier two ways to go. He must always take away one path, then make the tackle. For example, he can take away the running back's possibility of cutting left by being on that side of the back. Then he takes an angle at the ball carrier, knowing that he can go only to the right.

XVIII. Punt and Kick Catching Fundamentals

Running, throwing, and kicking are natural types of play for most children. Punting is something kids often do by themselves. They can become very good at it on their own, but they will get even better with instruction.

Punting

The stance of the punter is to lean slightly forward with the feet parallel or with the kicking foot slightly forward. The legs should be shoulder width, with the weight on the balls of the feet. The punter should be ready to move right or left in the event of a bad snap. The hands should give the snapper a low target, just inside the kicking leg knee.

Punters naturally want to hold out their hands as a target at chest or shoulder height, but they should hold them low to account for the snapper's natural tendency to snap the ball too high. A small error in the height of the snap can be critical. The least of the problems it causes is to throw off the timing of the punter's kick.

Equipment is crucial to the punter. The hip pads should not restrict hip movement. Low cut shoes should be worn to enable maximum ankle extension. Many professionals remove the tongue of the shoe and kick without a sock, because they do not want shock absorbing materials between the football and the bones of the foot. Most tie their shoelaces on the inside of the shoe so that the knot is not at the point where the ball makes contact with the foot.

Punting barefoot reduces the shock absorbing material between the ball and the foot. It also enables maximum ankle extension. However, it doesn't really make much difference in the kick. It is more of a psychological factor.

Punting sequence.

Adjusting the ball is the first thing the punter does. The laces are adjusted to the right, to a "one o'clock" position, for right-footed kickers, as the first step is taken with the kicking leg. Both the laces and the valve are "dead spots" that should not hit the foot. This is very important, because the punter's foot drives halfway into the ball on contact, and the more the ball is compressed the faster it bounces off the foot. Kicking a dead spot reduces the reaction of the ball off the foot. The punter should keep the ball out away from his body from the catch to the kick.

The first step is with the kicking leg. It is a short step made as the ball is being adjusted.

The second step is a normal length step. During this step the punter makes the final adjustments to the ball and prepares it for the drop. Beginning punters often adjust the ball and then start forward. This wastes several tenths of a second, which can be the difference between getting a kick off or having it blocked. Most punters angle the ball slightly inward and downward so that it spirals better. The inward angle should have the front end of the ball over the big toe or slightly outside it. Punters learn the best angle through experience.

Some coaches prefer that the ball is held so that it is pointed directly upfield with the longitudinal axis of the ball bisecting the laces of the shoe. This will often give an end-over-end kick that should bounce farther.

During this second step the ball will be brought up to chest height or lower and held away from the body. The ball should not be lifted or lowered from this chest height position. The head should be down with the eyes on the ball.

At the finish of this step the kicking leg is starting forward. The ball is dropped during this forward whip of the kicking leg. The body must continue to lean forward.

The drop is the most important part of the punt. Without the correct drop the ball will not hit the foot correctly. The punter should experiment with different methods of holding the ball so that it drops consistently. One constant is that the ball should be dropped as short a distance as possible. The longer the ball is in the air, the more mistakes in the drop are magnified. Windy conditions magnify the mistakes even more.

Most coaches teach that the kicking side hand be near the back of the ball with the other hand being forward. Some coaches prefer that the hands be under the ball with the hands sliding out from under it on the drop. Other coaches prefer to have the rear hand on top of the ball so that less contact with the ball is possible after the initial release. Their thinking is that with a hand under the ball the releasing hand may pull the ball with it to the outside as it releases. Players should experiment to find out which method they like best.

The ball should be dropped from a spot over where the kicking leg will swing. It should not be dropped from the center of the body. This would require that the punter kick toward that spot rather than having a free swinging, straight leg action.

A punter with a "quick" leg can drop the ball from a lower point. A punter with a slow leg must drop it from a higher position in order to get the ball to the foot at the proper spot. For a higher punt, hold the ball higher and closer to the body. For a lower punt, such as one into the wind, the ball should be held lower and farther from the body.

The kicking action starts with the kicking leg back. It is whipped forward through the ball. The kicking foot is extended so that the top of the foot continues in a straight line from the lower leg.

For most punts, the ball should be contacted just below knee level. This should give the punt good height. In cold weather, it should be contacted higher because the ball does not compress as much upon impact and leaves the foot quicker. The height at which the ball is contacted determines the trajectory of the ball. If the ball is kicked high and short, it was met too far above the ground. Meeting it too high also generally reduces the time that the ball is on the foot. The kicking leg may also be nearly fully extended if the ball is met too high. Both of these factors affect the amount of force imparted to the ball.

Taking the snap.

The follow-through should be as high as possible. If the kicking leg is stopped quickly, the leg slows down as the ball is contacted, thus taking speed off the ball. The force of the kicking action tends to give the body a rotating motion, forcing the kicking leg to finish on the opposite side of the body. This must be eliminated or minimized for maximum efficiency.

To practice dropping the ball for punts, players can simply drop the ball without kicking it. When the ball hits the ground, it should bounce back past the kicking foot and to the outside. This shows that the ball has been angled in and that the nose was slightly lower than the back end.

Taking the snap is something players must practice with a partner. The punter should provide the snapper with a low target. Putting the hands just inside the kicking knee is a good spot. Centers often snap too high in a game, so the low target allows for a high snap by the center. If the kicker places his hands at chest level, where he really wants the ball, an oversnap of two or three feet can be disastrous and can result in a blocked kick. However, with a target at knee height, a snap two or three feet too high will be at chest height.

The kicker then must get in front of the ball and look the ball into his hands. He then makes the adjustment of the laces to the one o'clock position and starts the forward steps.

Getting Used to Bad Snaps

Punters can learn how to deal with bad snaps by moving in front of the ball. If the ball is snapped to the punter's right, he steps to the right with the right foot and then moves the left foot to the right and re-establishes the correct stance. Punters should always move their entire body in front of the ball, rather than reaching out to the side for it.

If the ball is snapped too high, the punter should back up and reach for it. If it is way too high, the punter must turn and run after it. The punter should then run away from the opponents and kick the ball. If he is certain that it would be blocked, he should just run with it.

Hang time of over four seconds is essential for older players if the team is covering the kick, rather than kicking it out of bounds. For the Pop Warner level, a 25-yard kick should have a hang time of 2.5 seconds.

Individual differences account for some variation in technique. A punter with shorter arms probably needs to hold the ball closer to its end. The long-armed player may hold it more in the middle. The punter with less ankle flexibility may need a greater angle of the ball to the foot so that the toe does not contact the ball and create an end-over-end punt.

Angling the punt to the "coffin corner" is done by turning the body toward the target after catching the snap. The point of aim is determined by whether the punt drifts after it is kicked. A good punt will go straight. Some punters, however, get a drift. This drift is usually to the side of the punting leg, so a right-footed punter may get a drift to the right. If so, his target will not be in line with the arc of his kicking leg. Punters for whom this drift is common can aim at the point where the goal line and side line meet. A right-footed punter will aim to the goal line-side line intersection on his right. If his kick generally drifts five yards to the right, it will go out at about the five-yard line. A lower punt generally goes straighter to the target and varies less in the wind.

Another method of teaching punters how to aim is to put one or two markers on the ground, such as pieces of white athletic training tape. Punters can look for them as they make their steps. These markers should be placed where the feet will land as they step into the punt.

The pooch punt is aimed down the middle of the field. It may be fair-caught at the 10-yard line or allowed to bounce by the receiver and downed by the punting team. The pooch punt is easier to teach, especially if the punter is not a specialist and has limited time to practice kicking. The punt is kicked high to allow the coverage to get down under the punt and force the fair catch, or down the ball before it goes into the end zone. The ball should be held with the nose up and kicked with the toe up. This increases the chance of the ball bouncing straight up after it hits the ground. This type of bounce reduces the possibility that the ball will bounce into the end zone.

The depth of the punter should be 10 yards behind the line of scrimmage in the tight punt formation, 12 or 14 yards for a high school spread punt, and 15 yards for a college spread punt. Youth teams, of course, should shorten the distances relative to the age of their players.

Time of the punt depends on the distance between the punter and the snapper. Generally, the time taken in a game is less than that taken in practice because the snap is faster and the punter quicker.

Drills for the Punter

1. Force the punter to contend with poor snaps. Even during full team punting situations, the coach should occasionally (once each day) signal the snapper to snap high or low, left or right.
2. Time the punt with a snapper (1.9 seconds or less if 13 yards back) and without a snapper (1.1 seconds or less).
3. Aim punts for the side lines. Punters should aim at the goal line if a right-footed punter is punting to the right and aim at the 12- yard line if a right footed punter is kicking to the left "coffin corner."
4. "Pooch" punt to the 12-yard line.

Catching the Kicked Ball

The kick receiver must learn to adjust to the kicked ball, particularly the high kicked ball. The ball often goes farther than it appears it will go. Because of this, the inexperienced returner might misjudge the ball and let it go over his head.

When catching the ball, the returner must keep his elbows in close to the body so that if he misses the catch with his hands, his elbows can still secure the ball. If the elbows are wide, a missed ball will go right through the arms. The ball should be caught in the hands and then brought down to the ball-carrying position in the crook of the elbow with the hand cupped over the end of the ball. The receiver can then look up and start to run.

If fair-catching the ball, the receiver must wave his hand overhead. He should be clear in his intention. Occasionally a returner puts up his hand to shield his eyes from the sun and inadvertently signals for a fair catch.

The returner's job is to make certain that he catches the ball. If he fumbles, the kicking team probably will recover it, which amounts to about a 35-yard gain for the kicking team. If the returner lets it go over his head, the kicking team may gain another 10 to 20 yards on the kick. After the returner has caught the ball, he can start his return and hope to gain additional yardage. But the major concern is to catch the ball!

The fair catch signal.

XIX. Placekicking Fundamentals

The placekick can be used to score extra points, field goals, and to kick off.

The older style of placekicking was the straight-ahead kick. This enhances accuracy, but does not provide the distance that the more popular soccer style kick does. The soccer style kick enables a player to get longer leg whip prior to the kick, increased power from the hip rotation, and more foot into the ball.

The hold for the kick is usually made from a point seven-and-a-half to eight yards behind the snapper. Youth teams facing taller defenders should make the kick from eight yards back to reduce the possibility of a block. This is particularly true when kicking off of grass and for soccer style kickers who don't get the quick lift of the ball that straight-ahead kickers get. It is dangerous to make the kick too far behind the line of scrimmage, however, because the defensive ends have a greater chance of blocking the ball.

The holder should be on one knee, with the down knee closest to the center. The other leg is flexed and near the armpit closest to the kicker. The cleats under the toe should be on the ground so that the holder can stand up if necessary to handle a bad snap or to move out if a fake kick is called. The hand closest to the kicker may touch the target (tee or spot on the grass), and the other hand provides the target for the snapper (about a foot off the ground and slightly in front of the knee which is on the ground).

As the ball is caught, the holder must turn the laces forward so that they do not affect the flight of the ball after it is kicked. Laces to the side may make the ball drift in that direction. Laces at the rear may affect the kick if the kicker's foot contacts them. The hold is done with one finger of either hand.

In holding for a soccer style kicker whose kicks drift, the holder and kicker can experiment with holding the ball at an angle. By holding the top of the ball in the direction opposite the drift of the ball, the drift may be negated. So, for a right-footed kicker whose ball drifts left, the top of the ball can be held to the right. A properly kicked ball will not drift. If the wind is a factor, the holder can tilt the top of the ball into the wind about an inch. This helps offset the effect of the wind.

The kicker must experiment to find an exact starting point for the stance. Most kickers walk three normal steps straight back from the ball and then take two small steps (about two to two-and-a-half feet each) to the side, the side away from the kicking foot. This puts them at a 30-degree angle to the ball. From this point, the kicker may step up or back another foot to get to the precise spot where he feels the most comfortable in his approach to the ball. If the kicker starts too far away from the ball, greater than a 30-degree angle, the ball generally slices to the right. If the kicker isn't far enough over laterally, less than a 30-degree angle to the ball, the kick generally hooks to the left.

Most kickers assume a stance with the kicking foot back. This gives them two long steps into the kick. But kickers should use whatever stance is most comfortable to them. The head should be down and the eyes on the target — the tee.

The holder's stance.

As the holder catches the ball, the kicker steps forward with the non-kicking foot. This step can be as short as six inches. The next step is a long step with the kicking leg and the next step is with the non-kicking foot, with the foot landing even with the ball. The exact spot depends on the kicker. Most kickers land with the instep or the heel of the foot even with the ball. It is essential that the non-kicking foot be aligned with the desired flight of the ball. The toes should be pointing at the target — the middle of the goalpost or a wider target if a crosswind is expected to affect the flight of the ball.

The foot plant of the non-kicking foot should be six to eight inches to the side of the ball. If kicking off the grass, the toe should be six to eight inches ahead of the ball. If kicking from a two-inch tee, the toe should be two to four inches forward of the tee. This placement varies a bit from kicker to kicker.

The correct placement of the non-kicking foot is essential to an accurate kick. Right-footed kickers can look for mistakes in foot placement by following these cues:

- If the ball hooks left (to the right for left-footers), the foot probably is too close to the ball.
- If it slices to the right (to the left for left-footers), the anchored foot is too far from the ball.
- If the kick is too low, the planted foot is too far back or the body is leaning backward.

The Soccer Style Kick

This kick demands correct placement of the non-kicking foot to ensure accuracy, so it must be practiced continually. The player must adjust the starting point and the angle of approach until the kicking foot's plant is perfect every time. The kicking leg swings down through the ball, contacting it about one-and-a-half inches below the center. The toes must be pointed down (ankle extended) throughout the arc of the kicking leg's downward swing. The knee should extend quickly. More experienced kickers can improve the distance of their kicks by whipping the leg more quickly.

The body must remain forward to obtain maximum power. The eyes must be on the ball. The body must lean forward throughout the kicking action. Being straight up or leaning backward causes a hook or a low kick.

To get more height when kicking off the grass, the kicker can bend the knee more forward and contact the ball with the top part of the instep. This gives a "nine iron" effect and lifts the ball quicker than when the ball is contacted with the inside part of the instep.

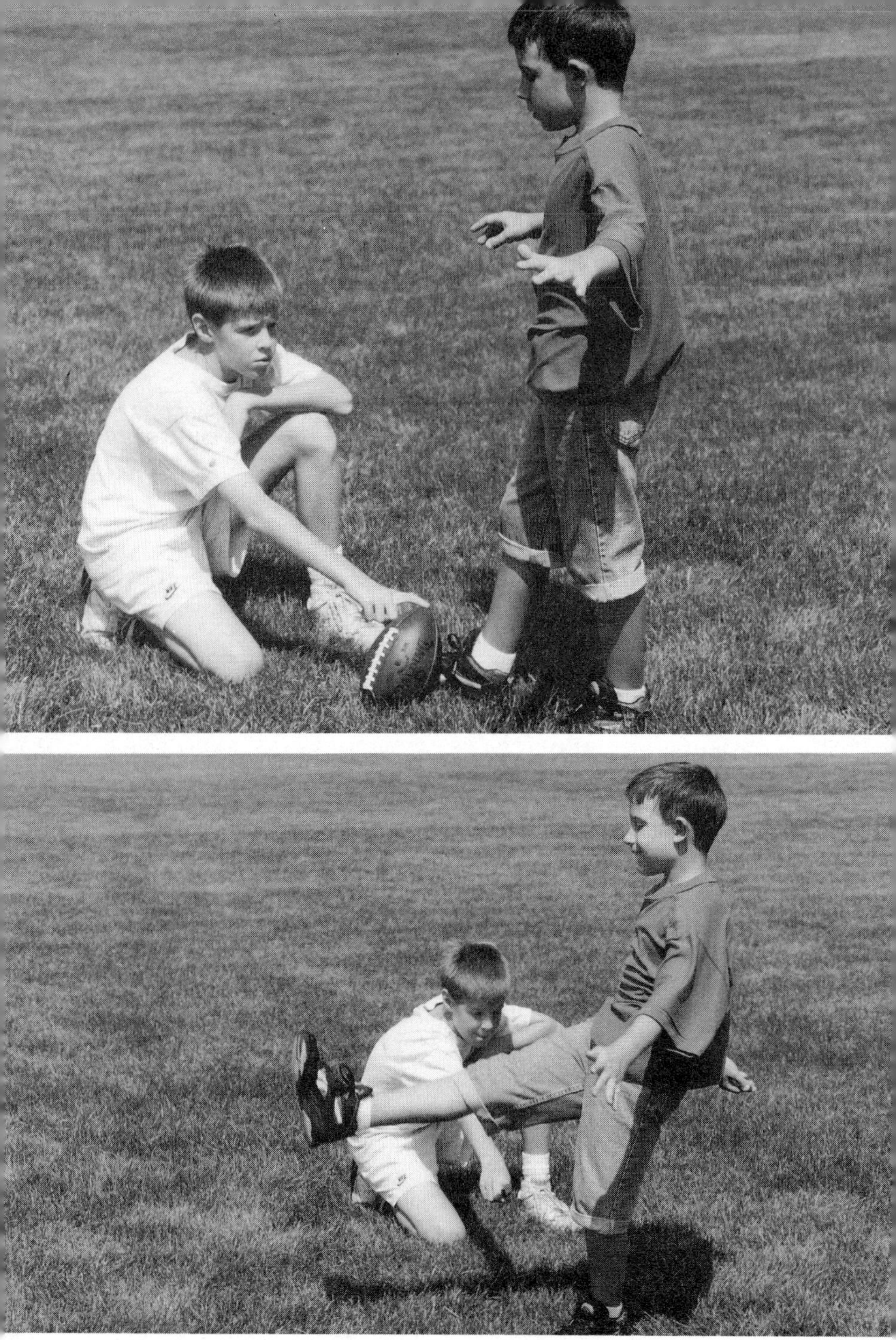

Placekicking sequence.

The follow-through should be straight toward the goal post. The more the body turns, the greater the chance of error. The follow-through should be high, to ensure full leg power and speed. The kicker should hop on the non-kicking foot as his body moves through the ball and as his leg follows through. The kick should be away in 1.4 to 1.5 seconds in practice. In games, it is generally about .1 second faster.

The Straight-ahead Kick

This kick is seldom used at the higher levels of play, but it tends to be more accurate, and therefore more appropriate for younger players. It also gets into the air more quickly, so it is harder to block. The disadvantage is that it is less likely to get the distance of the soccer style kick, but the longest field goal in NFL history, a 63-yarder by Tom Dempsey, was kicked in the straight-ahead style.

The kicking foot should be forward and the torso should be bent at the waist. The eyes must be on the target (tee). As the ball hits the holder's hands, the kicker should take a short step with the kicking foot. The step should be about one-foot long. (A longer step can generate more body speed and leg power, but it takes longer, so it is more likely result in a blocked kick or an error.)

The eyes must continue to focus on the target (the tee) as the steps are made. This eye contact must continue until the ball is kicked, then the eyes should follow the ball. Many coaches teach to keep watching the ground or the tee during the follow-through. This is wrong because it reduces the ability of the leg to follow-through, and it reduces the ability of the kicker to kick through the ball with the entire body. It is absolutely essential to kick with the whole body in every type of kick.

The second step is a long step. During this step, the kicking leg is swung back. The farther back it moves, the greater the power that can be generated. The non-kicking foot should land about four inches outside and eight to ten inches behind the ball. The exact distance depends on the height of the tee and the length of the kicker's leg. If kicking from the ground, the planted foot should be six to eight inches behind the ball for high school players. If using a two-inch tee, it should be eight to ten inches back. For smaller boys, it should be closer.

The eyes concentrate on the spot on the ball that is the kicker's target. This target should be one to one-and-a-half inches below the center of the ball. One inch is better, because more distance is possible. A lower target lifts the ball up quicker, but it reduces the distance of the kick.A hang time of four seconds is considered very good at any level of play. Young kickers, of course, will not come close to this level.

For soccer style kicks from a two-inch tee, the kicker's foot plant should be six to eight inches to the side of the tee and two to four inches behind it. From a one-inch tee, the toe should be two to four inches in front of the ball. This varies slightly from kicker to kicker. The ball is kicked just below the center of the ball.

The thigh comes forward as the abdominal muscles and hip flexors contract. The knee extensors straighten the leg as the ball is kicked. Depending on the speed of the leg, the toe of the kicker's foot may go as deep as three to four inches into the ball. The ball will stay on the toe from the time it is contacted until it is 12 to 18 inches off the ground. The greater the speed of the leg, the greater distance the ball remains on the foot.

The foot must remain locked at a 90-degree angle from the time it starts forward until the follow-through is completed. It must not vary from this 90-degree angle until the ball has left the foot. (Some kickers tie a shoelace from the bottom lace to the ankle to keep the foot up. This requires an adjustment in the step and the hold, so it is not recommended.)

The foot should also remain parallel to the line of the arc of the kicking leg. Even one degree off of the parallel can create a twist of the leg or ankle when the ball is contacted. This reduces the power and accuracy of the kick. The muscles that control the twist (rotation) of the thigh and the rotation of the ankle must be strong enough to overcome the torque that could be created at the instant of the contact of the foot with the ball. The leg should continue up and through the ball and finish as close as possible to the kicking-side shoulder. After the kick, the kicker should land on the non-kicking foot.

Kickoffs

The kickoff can be done with the soccer style or the straight-ahead style of kick. Because the soccer style kick usually results in greater distance, it is generally preferred, particularly for kickoffs. The objective for high school and college kickers is to kick the ball consistently inside the 10-yard line with a hang time of four seconds.

The soccer style kicker should start 10 yards back and five yards to the side. The straight-ahead kicker should start at the tee and then run back toward the goal line until he feels comfortable and kick an imaginary ball. The point where he makes his kick would be the proper starting point. It generally will be eight to 10 yards from the ball for a high school player, and shorter for a younger player.

This approach is used for either style of kick, straight-ahead or soccer. Some kickers feel comfortable with a few steps, but others want several. After the steps seem comfortable, they should be marked off with the traditional stepping method.

Soccer style kickoff.

The ball is generally teed up as straight as possible. However, individual preferences as to tilt can be considered. As the kicker approaches the ball, he generates more speed than with a field goal. Therefore, the strides will be longer and the kicking leg will follow through with a greater arc, thus generating more speed.

The kicking action is the same as described for the field goal — a quick leg snap. However, power is more important than accuracy in the kickoff. For this reason, the kicker must "attack" the ball with a very quick leg action. The whole body is used to kick, and both feet often leave the ground. After the follow-through, the kicker lands on his kicking foot.

As the ball is kicked, the hips and shoulders should be parallel to the goal line. If the ball hooks to the left (for right footers), the planted foot is probably too close to the ball. If it slices to the right, the foot is probably too far from it.

For straight-ahead kicks, the planted foot should be about four inches to the side of the ball. If kicking off the grass, it should be eight to ten inches behind it. Off a one-inch tee, 12 inches is about right, off a two-inch tee 14 inches, and from a three-inch tee 18 inches. The higher the tee, the greater the height and hang time possible. Younger children will be closer to the ball than the high school averages noted here.

If the kicker is told to aim toward a particular spot on the field (such as when kicking away from an outstanding returner), he should follow through into that area. As the follow through is completed, the kicker continues directly toward the ball and is the safetyman. Because of this additional duty, kickers must learn how to tackle.

The squib kick is used when a team wants to change the timing of a return or to reduce the possibility of a long return. It can also be used when a team does not have an effective kickoff man. The kick will not be long, probably landing between the 20- and 30-yard lines in high school ball, but it should be difficult to control and may well be fumbled by the receiver. For the squib kick, the ball is placed on its side with the long axis parallel to the goal line. The ball should be kicked to the side of the center so that it bounces unpredictably.

Onside Kickoffs

The kickoff specialist must know how to perform the onside kickoff. One method is simply to kick the ball softer about 12 to 15 yards downfield and then recover it.

Straight-ahead kickoff.

A second method is to kick high on the ball — the "tip off" kick. If properly done, this makes the ball take a short hop and then a high bounce that should enable the cover men to get to the ball and outnumber the receivers at the point where the ball comes down. This should be aimed at the sideline about 12 to 15 yards downfield.

A third method, the most difficult to perform, has the kicker punch the side of the ball, thus making it spin. If properly done, the ball spins past the 10-yard mark and then starts spinning back toward the kicking team. The ball moves like a top, with the spin creating a circular path of the ball.

Placekicking Drills

- All kickers, regardless of style, should practice from a very sharp angle to the goal posts. This makes the target very small. It forces the kicker to be much more aware of the importance of alignment and follow-through.
- Soccer-style kickers can kick a soccer ball continuously from a point four to five feet from a wall to get the proper feeling of the foot on the ball.

XX. The Mental Side of Football

Wishing won't make players become better. They must practice and learn the physical skills of football, and they must physically condition their bodies. However, they can also learn to become better players by practicing mentally.

Mental Practice

Championship athletes have known for years that mental practice helps performance. Only recently have sports psychologists refined methods of utilizing the mind's contribution to the game. Mental imagery, or visualization, is the name given to this type of mental practice. It can be done externally — by observing college or professional players in person or on a video tape, or by players imagining watching themselves from outside their bodies. The golfer Jack Nicklaus calls this "going to the movies." It can also be done internally — "feeling" yourself doing the action.

While mentally experiencing a skill, athletes can practice whatever aspect of that skill they want to improve. The following study illustrates the benefits of mental imagery. (Smith, Daniel Elon. *Evaluation of An Imagery Training Program With Intercollegiate Basketball Players.* Unpublished Doctoral Dissertation. University of Illinois at Urbana-Champaign. 1986. Pp.91-104.)

Basketball players were divided into two groups. The first group physically practiced 100 free throws per day, while the second group was placed in a dark, quiet room and told to imagine that they were successfully attempting 100 free throws. When the two groups were tested at the end of the study, the second group shot a better percentage. It is believed that when they were imagining the free throws, they were successful on 100 percent of their shots. The group that was actually shooting missed some of their shots in practice, which caused them not to be as confident when it came to the actual test.

Football players can imagine themselves doing everything correctly from start to finish, with a successful outcome. A quarterback, for example, should imagine himself competing in situations that are not ideal, such as in the rain, the wind, or the hot sun. By imagining these possibilities, he should be better prepared when actually facing such situations.

All players should imagine themselves doing specific skills, such as the following:

- stripping the ball from a ball carrier who is being tackled
- catching a hook pass while being hit from behind
- reading the blocking triangle
- playing the quarterback on an option play
- pass rushing against an agile blocker
- countering the pass rush as a blocker

The possibilities are endless. All players should practice mentally. It is more than dreaming about making a catch or a tackle, it is imagining the exact situation and doing it perfectly.

Relaxation is another essential facet of effective mental exercising. Players should practice taking a slow, deep breath before stepping into the huddle or before getting set for an offensive play. This can help clear the players' minds so they can concentrate on their bodies. Relaxed muscles are more prepared for the sustained movements essential to running or exploding into a block or tackle. Tense muscles tend to inhibit smooth, efficient activities, and speed up the onset of fatigue.

Players can get the most out of relaxation and deep breathing by sitting quietly with their eyes closed and concentrating on slowly taking and releasing deep breaths. They can say to themselves "breathe in, breathe out" or repeat a nonsense syllable such as "om" or "one." Concentrating on a one syllable repetition helps players relax by eliminating all tension-causing thoughts from their minds.

By "not thinking," as they concentrate on breathing, the players' muscles relax. If other thoughts come into their minds, they should return to their breathing pattern and verbal repetition. This is the basis for many of the benefits to be gained from the Hindu practice of meditation.

After players have learned to relax while sitting calmly in a quiet place, the next step is to transfer that ability to their workouts. The players should be relaxed whenever they practice mental imagery. They should also be able to relax when exercising, whether in a workout or a game. A relaxed body is more ready to react than a tense body.

Concentration is the third major area of mental practice. While working out, players may want to concentrate on breathing deeply, relaxing their arms in a stance, or exploding into a block. When concentrating on ideas in practice, players must always keep it positive, such as "exhale fully" or "I am relaxed." Negative thinking is counter-productive and causes stress. The runner who is thinking, "I had better not be stiff," is setting himself up for unnecessarily tightening up.

Quarterbacks should concentrate on the exact target for their passes. Receivers should concentrate on the spin of the ball and on the front tip of the ball. Blockers should concentrate on the first step of the block or the exact point of aim for the hands.

Goalsetting

Another important aspect of the mental side of sports, as well as of life, is setting both long-term and short-term goals. Short-term goals should assist in achieving long-term goals. After teams and players decide on long-term goals, they should make plans to achieve those goals. An example of a long-term goal is a desire to be the starting left guard next season.

Short-term goals involve improving specific skills to enable players to achieve a long-term goal. Examples of short-term goals are improving techniques or becoming faster or stronger.

A practice schedule should be designed to increase the players' chances of attaining those goals. If players want to increase their ability to catch or kick, they should be helped to select a workout at practice and at home that aids in achieving the goals. Team members also can include mental conditioning in trying to achieve their goals. They can visualize themselves moving faster or completing a longer workout, for example.

Glossary

Angle block — Blocking a player inside or outside who is not "on" or "shading" the blocker.

Arc block — A block on the defensive end or corner by a running back with the back attempting to block the defender in. The blocker starts wide for a few steps then attacks the defender.

Audible — Changing the offensive play at the line of scrimmage.

Backpedal — Running directly backward, a technique used by defensive backs and linebackers.

Blitz — A defensive play in which a linebacker or defensive back attacks past the LOS.

Bomb — A long pass.

Boot or bootleg — Quarterback fakes to backs going one way while he goes the opposite way to run or pass

Bump and run — A technique in which the defensive back hits the potential receiver on the line of scrimmage then (to slow his route) then runs with the receiver.

Chucking — Hitting a receiver before the pass is thrown.

Clip — A block in which the defender is hit from behind. It is illegal unless done in the legal clipping zone, close to the snapper (two to five yards from the ball, depending on the level of play.)

Cloud — A commonly used term which indicates that the cornerback will cover the outside flat zone on a pass.

Combo or combination block — A block in which linemen exchange responsibilities.

Corners or corner backs — The widest secondary players in an umbrella (4 deep) defense.

Counter — A play which ends going a different direction than the initial flow of the backs would indicate.

Crackback block — A block by an offensive player who has lined up more than two yards outside of the tackle and is blocking low on a man inside him. It is illegal.

Crossover step — A step by a lineman or back in which, when moving laterally, the player steps first with the foot away from the direction toward which he is traveling.

Curl — A pass pattern in which the receiver runs 15 to 20 yards downfield then comes back toward the passer in an open area of the defensive coverage.

Cut back — The movement of a ball carrier away from the direction he was originally running so that he can run behind the tacklers.

Cut block — A block aimed at the ankles or knees of the defender. It is illegal at some levels of play.

Cut off — A block in which a player blocks a player who is closer to the hole than is the offensive player.

Dash — A planned passing action in which the passer drops back then moves to his right or left in a planned action. The blockers move with him.

Defense — The team which is not in control of the ball.

Dime defense — A defense in which six defensive backs are in the game in order to stop a likely pass.

Dive — A quick straight ahead play with the halfback carrying the ball.

Dog or red dog — A linebacker attacking past the LOS at the snap of the ball.

Double cover — Two defenders covering one offensive receiver.

Double team — A block in which two offensive players block one defender.

Down — A play which begins after the ball is stopped. There are two types of downs, a scrimmage down and a free kick down.

Down block — Linemen block down towards center.

Down lineman — A defensive lineman.

Drag — A delayed pattern in which a tight end or a wideout runs a shallow pattern across the center.

Draw — A fake pass which ends with one of the backs carrying the ball after the defensive linemen are "drawn" in on the pass rush.

Drive block — A straight ahead block.

Drop — The action of the passer as he moves away from the line of scrimmage. Three, five, seven and nine step drops are common.

Eagle — A 5-2 defensive alignment with the tackles outside of the offensive guards and the linebackers on the ends.

Encroachment — Entering the neutral zone (the line of scrimmage bounded by both ends of the ball) before the ball is snapped. It is a penalty in high school football. At the college and pro level it is a penalty only if contact is made with the other team.

End around — A reverse play in which a tight end or a wide out carries the ball.

End zone — The ten yard area between the goal line and the end line.

Even defense — A defensive alignment in which there is no defensive lineman over the center.

Extra point — See "point after touchdown."

Fade — A pass pattern used generally against a man-to-man coverage in which the receiver runs deep and fades away from the defender.

Fair catch — The opportunity for a receiving player to catch a kicked ball and not be tackled. It is signaled by waving one arm overhead. The ball cannot be advanced after making a fair catch. The team has an opportunity to put the ball in play by a scrimmage down or a free kick down.

False block — Hitting an opposing lineman on the same side as you wish him to move, used against good reacting defensive lineman.

Far — A player who is aligned away from where the ball will be run or passed. The "far" guard may trap block or the "far" back may be the ball carrier.

Field goal — A ball place kicked or drop kicked over the goal posts. It scores three points.

Flanker — A back split wider than a wingback.

Flipper — A forearm shiver.

Flood — A pass pattern in which the offense sends more receivers into an area than there are defenders. It uses both a horizontal and a vertical stretch.

Flow — The apparent direction of the ball during a scrimmage play. Most plays attack in the direction of the flow. Counters, reverses, and throwback passes go against the flow.

Fold — A block in which an offensive lineman blocks the next defender on the line while the offensive lineman nearest that defender moves behind the blocker and blocks the near backer.

Forearm shiver (Forearm lift or rip) — A block protection technique in which the defender wards off the blocker by hitting and lifting him with his forearm.

Formation — The alignment of the offensive team. At least seven players must be within a foot of the line of scrimmage.

Forward pass — A pass thrown forward from behind the line of . scrimmage. College and pro teams are allowed only one forward pass per play. High schools are allowed multiple forward passes on one play.

Free kick down — A down in which the kicking team can tee up the ball to kick (as in a kick off) or can place kick or punt the ball after a safety. The defensive team must stay at least ten yards from the ball. Free kick downs occur after a touchdown or field goal. They can also occur after a safety (when the team scored against can have one scrimmage down or a free kick down in which it can kick the ball in any manner) or after a fair catch (in which the receiving team has the choice of a set of scrimmage downs or one free kick down in which it can score a field goal).

Free safety — The safety man opposite the power side of the offensive line (the tight end). He is usually free to cover deep zones.

Freeze option — A play in which an inside fake to one back running up the middle should freeze the linebackers. The play ends as an option play between the quarterback and another runner.

Front — The alignment of the defensive linemen.

Game plan — The offensive, defensive, and kicking strategy for an opponent.

Gap — The space between offensive or defensive linemen.

Gap defense — A defensive front with the defensive linemen in the offensive gaps.

Goal line — The area over the inside edge of the chalk mark which marks the end of the playing field. The ten yard end zone is beyond the goal line.

Guards — The offensive linemen on either side of the center.

Hand shiver — A defensive block protection in which the defender hits the blocker with his hands and extends his arms to keep the blocker away from his body.

Hang time — The amount of time a kick stays in the air.

Hash marks — Short lines parallel with the sidelines which intersect each five yard mark on the field. They are 1/3 of the way in from the sideline (18 2/3 yards) for high school and college and even with the goal posts for the pro game. Every play starts from a point on or between the hash marks

Hitch — A quick pattern to a wide receiver in which he drives off the line then stops.

Hitting position — A balanced "ready position" in which the weight is on the balls of the feet, the knees are flexed, the torso is flexed forward, and the head is up.

Hook block — A block in which the offensive blocker must get outside of a defender who is outside of him, then block that defender in.

Hook pattern — A pass pattern in which the receiver runs downfield, stops, then comes back toward the passer.

Horizontal stretch — Forcing the pass defenders to cover the entire width of the field on a pass.

Hot receiver — A receiver who becomes open because the defender who would have covered him has stunted into the offensive backfield. The receiver yells "hot" when he sees he will be open and the passer passes quickly to him.

I formation — A formation in which the quarterback, fullback, and tailback are in a line.

Influence — Getting an opponent to move in the direction desired through finesse.

Inside slot — A slot back aligned close to the tight lineman.

Invert — A four deep defensive alignment in which the safeties are closer to the LOS than the corners. They are expected to quickly assist in run support.

Jam — Hitting a potential receiver before the ball is released by the passer.

Key — Watching an opponent to determine what he or his team will be doing.

Lateral pass — A pass thrown parallel with the LOS or backward. It can be thrown overhand or underhand.

Lead — An offensive player goes through the hole and leads the ball carrier, usually looking to the inside to pick up a backer.

Lead step — A step with the foot closest to the direction toward which the player is moving.

Line of scrimmage — An area approximately a foot wide (the width of the ball) which stretches from sideline to sideline.

Load — A block in which an offensive player coming from the inside blocks a wide defender on a wide play. The blocker will have his head and shoulders on the offensive side of the defender and the play is designed to go around him.

Loop — A defensive lineman's move from a gap to a man, a man to a gap, or sometimes from a man to another man.

LOS — Line of scrimmage.

M4M — An abbreviation for man-for-man pass defense.

Mac — Middle linebacker (mac means "middle back").

Mike — Middle guard or "nose man" (Mike means "middle in").

Misdirection — A play which goes against the flow of the play, such as a bootleg, reverse, or throwback.

Muff — A mistake in catching the ball on a kicking play.

Near — The player aligned close to the point of attack. So the "near" guard may trap or the near back may be the ball carrier.

Neutral zone — The area bounded by each end of the ball which extends from sideline to sideline and from the ground to the sky. Only the snapper can be in that zone before the ball is snapped.

Nickel defense — A defense with five defensive backs.

Nose guard or nose tackle — A defensive lineman playing on the offensive center.

Odd defense — A defense which has a man on the offensive snapper. This will result in a defensive line with an odd number of players on it.

Offside — Side of the line away from where the play will attack.

Off tackle play — A play which hits in the area of the offensive tackle and end.

Offense — The team controlling the ball.

Okie — The Oklahoma 5-2 defense (Linebackers over the offensive guards).

On side — Side of the line to which the play will attack.

On side kick — A short kickoff which travels at least ten yards which can then be recovered by either team.

Option play — A play in which the quarterback runs at a wide defender forcing the defender to either tackle him or stop the pitch to a trailing back. QB can keep or pitch.

Overshift — The alignment of the defensive linemen one man closer to the strength of the formation.

Pass pattern — The path or route that a receiver runs in attempting to get open.

Passing tree — The potential routes which a receiver can run. When drawn together they resemble a tree.

Penetration — The movement across the line of scrimmage by the defenders.

Pick — A pass pattern in which one of the potential receivers hits or screens off a defender allowing his teammate to be free. It is used primarily against a man to man defense. It is illegal to hit a defensive back before the ball is caught but it is legal to create a screen by stopping (as in a hook pattern) or having the receivers cross close to each other.

Place kick — A kick in which the ball is either held by a player or held by a tee. It is used for kick offs, field goals, and points after touchdowns.

Play action — A pass off of a run fake

Pocket — The area surrounding a passer which is being protected by his blockers.

Point after touchdown (P.A.T.) — An extra play allowed after a touchdown in which the team has an opportunity to make one point by kicking the ball through over the goal posts or two points by running or passing the ball over the goal line (high school and college game only). Ball is spotted at the three yard line for this play.

Pre-snap read — A cue read by the quarterback or receivers based on the alignment of the pass defenders.

Prevent defense — A defense sometimes used by a team which is ahead late in a half. It uses extra defensive backs playing deeper than usual and fewer than normal pass rushers.

Primary receiver — The first choice of the passer in a pass pattern.

Pull — The movement of an offensive lineman behind the line as he leads the play.

Punt — A kick made on a scrimmage down which is designed to make the most yardage when possession is changed.

Pursuit — The movement of the defensive players to get them to a spot where they can make the tackle.

Quick count — A snap count which gets the ball in play quicker than normal, hoping to catch the defensive team unprepared.

Quick side — The side of the offensive line away from the strong side.

Reach block — An offensive lineman blocking a defender who is closer to the point of attack than himself or a tight end getting outside position on a backer who is slightly outside of him.

Read — Getting an idea of what the opponents are doing by looking at one or more of them as the play develops. It can be done by defenders watching offensive linemen or backs or by passers and receivers watching pass coverage defenders.

Reduced front — A defensive lineman playing closer to the center than normal. An example would be a tackle playing on the guard rather than on the offensive tackle.

Release — The movement of a receiver in leaving the line of scrimmage.

Reverse — A play in which a wide player on one side runs the ball against the flow of the other backs.

Rollout — A deep, generally wide, path of the quarterback behind the other backs.

Rove — See dash.

Rover — A defensive back who can be given various assignments. He is usually playing in a defense which has a 5-2 front and three defensive backs.

Run force — The responsibility of a defender to make the runner commit to an inside or outside path once he has passed the offensive end.

Sack — The tackling of the passer before he has a chance to pass.

Safety — A two-point play which occurs when an offensive player is tackled behind his own end zone.

Safetyman — The defensive back or backs with the deepest responsibility.

Scoop — A block in which a lineman blocks the next defensive man to the play side this releases the next lineman out to block a backer.

Scramble — The running of the quarterback after he has been forced out of the pocket on a pass play.

Scrape — The path of a linebacker who is moving into the offensive line—usually on a key.

Screen — A pass, usually behind the LOS, after a deep drop by the quarterback. Some linemen pull to lead the receiver.

Scrimmage down — One of four attempts of the offense to advance the ball ten yards and make another first down.

Seams — The areas between the defensive zones which are more likely to be open to complete passes.

Secondary — The safetymen and cornerbacks.

Set — The offensive or defensive alignment.

Set up — The last step of a quarterback's drop—the spot from which he would like to pass.

Shading — The defender is not head up on the blocker but part of his body overlaps the body of the offensive player.

Shift — A change of alignment from one set to another before the snap of the ball. It can be used by the offensive or the defensive team.

Shiver — A defensive technique used to protect the defender from the block. It can be done with the hands or the forearms contacting the blocker.

Short list — The list of plays most likely to be used in a game with plays listed according to each situation.

Shotgun — A formation in which the quarterback sets several yards behind the center to be able to see the field better on a pass play. More wide receivers are also used. Some runs will be made from this formation to keep the defense honest.

Shuffle — The path of a linebacker who is moving nearly parallel with the LOS as he diagnoses the play and determines how he will attack the ball carrier.

Signals — Offensive or defensive code words which tell the team which alignment and which play to use. Also the cadence called by the quarterback to get the play started.

Sky — A term used in pass coverage to indicate that a safety will cover a short flat zone.

Slant — As a defensive lineman it is a hard move usually from an offensive lineman into a gap, as an offensive term it is a pass pattern, usually by a wide receiver, angling in toward the center of the field.

Slip block — Same as scoop.

Slot — A back lined up in the area between a split end and the tackle.

Snap — The act of putting the ball in play. It can be handed to the quarterback or thrown (between the legs or to the side) to a back.

Snapper — The offensive lineman who puts the ball in play, usually the center.

Spearing — An illegal action in which a player drives his head into a player, usually a player on the ground.

Speed option — An option play in which there is no inside fake. All backs run wide immediately.

Sprint draw — A draw play off of a sprint out move by the quarterback.

Sprint out — A fast and shallow path of the quarterback

Spy — Keeping a defender near the line of scrimmage on pass plays in order to stop a draw play or a run by the quarterback.

Squib kick — A low flat kickoff which is difficult to handle. It is often used when the receiving team has an effective kick returner or when the kicking team does not have a long ball kicker.

Stack — Playing a linebacker directly behind a defensive lineman.

Streak — A pass pattern in which the receiver runs long and fast.

Stretch — To widen the defense by placing offensive men in wide positions.

Strong safety — The safety on the strong side (tight end) of the offense.

Strong side — The side of the offensive line which blocks for the power plays. Usually the side of the tight end is designated the strong side.

Stunt — A defensive maneuver in which linemen create a hole for a backer to move through the line or a movement between defensive linemen which will allow at least one to penetrate the LOS.

Sweep — A wide offensive power running play.

Tight end — A receiver playing close to the offensive tackle.

Touchback — A play which ends behind the receiver's goal line but in which the impetus of the ball was generated by the other team. There is no score. The ball is moved to the 20 yard line for the first down.

Trap — Blocking a defensive lineman by an offensive player who did not line up close to him originally. In a trap block the blocker will have his head on the defensive (downfield) side of the opponent and the play is designed to go inside the block.

Triangle — Triple key for a defensive player. A blocking triangle involves the three most dangerous blockers who could attack him. For a linebacker it would involve one or two linemen and one or two backs.

Twist — A movement between defensive linemen, especially in a pass situation, in which the linemen cross hoping that at least one will get clear into the backfield.

Two minute offense or two minute drill — The attack used by a team late in a half when they are behind and attempting to score while conserving time.

Umbrella — A secondary four deep alignment usually with the corners closer to the LOS than the safeties.

Unbalanced line — An offensive alignment in which four or more linemen are set on one side of the line of scrimmage.

Undershift — A defensive alignment in which the defensive linemen have moved a man away from their normal position away from the strength of the offensive formation.

Uprights — The vertical poles which hold up the cross bar of the goal posts.

Vertical stretch — Forcing the pass defenders to cover deep even if the pass is in the short or intermediate zones.

Waggle — A pass action off a running play in which the quarterback moves wide and deep after faking to a back. Some coaches call it a waggle if the quarterback move in the direction of the flow behind the backs to whom he has faked. Others call it a waggle if he moves opposite the flow and is protected by a pulling lineman.

Walkaway — A position taken by a linebacker or defensive back between a wide receiver and the offensive linemen. It allows the defender to be in position to stop the quick slant pass and still be able to play a wide run.

Weak side — The side of the offense away from the tight end.

Wedge — A block in which three or more players block an area.

Wide out — A split end or flanker.

Wide receiver — See wide out.

Wing — A back lined up outside a tight end (usually a yard outside and a yard back).

Zone blocking — Pass protection blockers protect an area rather than blocking a specific man. It is used against stunting defenses.

Zone defense — A pass coverage in which the linebackers and defensive backs protect areas and play the ball rather than watch specific men.

Epilogue...for fathers

We know that football is a very special game in many ways. Most importantly, perhaps, it is a great way for fathers to get closer to their sons and to help their sons be successful in an area that is important to the young men, especially for teen-agers in middle school and high school. Developing self esteem is very important for young people, and having a close relationship with a parent and being a successful athlete can give a boy a feeling of positive self worth and a sense of accomplishment. Whether you work with your son in understanding the game on television or by coaching his youth football team, you will be getting closer to him and helping him to enjoy life more. By taking the time to read this book, you are obviously a concerned and loving father. We salute you and wish you the best!

About the Authors

Tom Flores has been the Seattle Seahawks President and General Manager since 1989 and the head coach since 1992. He enters his 33rd year in the National Football League in 1993. Flores is one of only two people in NFL history, along with former Chicago Bears' head coach Mike Ditka, to have a Super Bowl ring as a player, assistant coach, and head coach.

Bob O'Connor has been a football coach for 40 years at every level of play: junior high, high school, junior college, college, semi-pro, and European football. A professor at Pierce College, O'Connor has also been the author of 17 books on health, sports, and physical education topics.